AF797320

PAT BROWN, MBA

# GymnasticsMoney101

*Using Gymnastics to Teach the Basics of Money*

ABRAM · 47 · BROWN

*First published by AbramBrown47 2026*

*Copyright © 2026 by Pat Brown, MBA*

*All rights reserved. No part of this publication may be reproduced, stored, or transmitted in any form or by any means, electronic, mechanical, photocopying, recording, scanning, or otherwise without written permission from the publisher. It is illegal to copy this book, post it to a website, or distribute it by any other means without permission.*

*This novel is entirely a work of fiction. The names, characters, and incidents portrayed in it are the work of the author's imagination. Any resemblance to actual persons, living or dead, events, or localities is entirely coincidental.*

*Pat Brown, MBA asserts the moral right to be identified as the author of this work.*

*Pat Brown, MBA has no responsibility for the persistence or accuracy of URLs for external or third-party Internet Websites referred to in this publication and does not guarantee that any content on such Websites is, or will remain, accurate or appropriate.*

*Designations used by companies to distinguish their products are often claimed as trademarks. All brand names and product names used in this book and on its cover are trade names, service marks, trademarks, and registered trademarks of their respective owners. The publishers and the book are not associated with any product or vendor mentioned in this book. None of the companies referenced within the book have endorsed the book.*

*First edition*

*ISBN: 978-1-967737-53-6*

*This book was professionally typeset on Reedsy.*
*Find out more at reedsy.com*

# Contents

# Foreword

Gymnastics teaches lessons that last far beyond the gym.

Before most athletes ever think about money, gymnasts learn balance. They learn patience. They learn that small errors compound quickly and that execution matters just as much as difficulty. They learn that chasing perfect scores without control leads to falls, deductions, and missed potential.

Those lessons are exactly why this book exists.

I have worked with athletes for decades, both during their competitive years and long after the chalk has settled. The pattern is consistent. Gymnasts are some of the most disciplined, detail-oriented, and mentally tough people you will ever meet. Yet many of them feel overwhelmed, anxious, or behind when it comes to money.

That disconnect is not a character flaw. It is a coaching gap.

Gymnastics is one of the most structured environments imaginable. Training schedules are precise. Routines are broken down into parts. Form is corrected relentlessly. Accountability is constant. When you are competing, someone is always watching. Judges score every movement. Coaches review every rep. Progress is measured clearly.

Then one day, that structure disappears.

No one sets your financial schedule.

No one reviews your spending film.

No one explains how income, savings, investing, and protection fit together.

No one warns you that perfectionism, one of your greatest strengths in the gym, can quietly sabotage your financial life.

You are expected to figure it out on your own.

Gymnastics Money 101 exists to rebuild structure where it was never installed.

This is not a traditional money book. It does not rely on fear, hype, or technical jargon. It does not assume you want to become a financial expert. It assumes something far more realistic.

It assumes you know how to train.

It assumes you respect fundamentals.

It assumes you understand that long-term success comes from consistency, not shortcuts.

Money, like gymnastics, rewards clean execution. You do not need the hardest routine if you cannot land it. You do not need the flashiest investment if it introduces unnecessary risk. Difficulty adds value only when it is controlled.

Throughout this book, you will see financial concepts explained through the lens of gymnastics because that is the language you already speak. Budgeting becomes balance. Saving becomes injury protection. Investing becomes routine construction. Risk becomes difficulty selection. Mistakes become deductions. Long-term success becomes sticking the landing.

The goal is not perfection.

The goal is stability, control, and confidence.

This book is especially important for gymnasts because of how early the sport demands sacrifice. Many gymnasts give up normal teenage jobs, social routines, and financial exposure in pursuit of excellence. That tradeoff makes sense competitively, but it often delays basic financial education. When income eventually shows up, whether through a career, coaching, college opportunities, or entrepreneurship, the system to manage it is missing.

Without a system, even disciplined people struggle.

Gymnastics Money 101 is your system.

You will not be told to chase perfect scores. You will be taught how to build a routine that holds up under pressure. You will not be told to avoid risk entirely. You will be taught how to choose difficulty intelligently. You will not be told that one great decision fixes everything. You will be taught how small habits compound over time.

Most importantly, you will be reminded of something gymnastics already taught you.

Progress is built when nobody is watching.

Details matter even when the crowd is quiet.

Confidence comes from preparation, not hope.

You finish strong because you trained to finish strong.

Whether you are still competing, transitioning out of the sport, coaching, or building the next chapter of your life, this book is meant to meet you where you are. It is not about what you should have known earlier. It is about what you can execute now.

Money does not care how talented you are.

It cares how consistently you show up.

Gymnastics taught you how to do hard things the right way. This book simply applies those lessons to a different arena.

The routine is not over.

Now it is time to stick the landing.

# Introduction

Every gymnast remembers a routine like this.

The mount is clean. The first pass is solid. Connections are sharp. The difficulty is there. The crowd is quiet in that way that means they are paying attention. Halfway through, you know you are on pace for something special. Your coach knows it too.

Then it happens.

A step on a landing.

A balance check.

A rushed connection.

Or worse, a fall at the very end.

The score flashes, and suddenly none of the earlier perfection feels like it mattered as much as it should have.

That is gymnastics reality. Scores reward the full routine, not just the hardest skills. Difficulty matters, but execution and the finish decide everything. You can do ninety percent of a routine right and still walk away disappointed if you do not stick the landing.

Money works the same way.

Most people think financial success is about big moments. A high-paying job. A great investment. A lucky break. A single perfect decision. That mindset mirrors chasing perfect scores without respecting consistency, control, and endurance.

The truth is simpler and harder at the same time.

Financial success is a full routine.

And most people do not fail on the opening skills. They fail at the end.

## *Why Gymnasts Are Especially Vulnerable Financially*

Gymnasts are trained to focus intensely on the present moment. One skill at a time. One routine at a time. One meet at a time. That focus is a strength in competition. Financially, it can create blind spots.

Many gymnasts do everything right early in life.

They work hard.

They delay gratification.

They sacrifice normal experiences.

They show discipline most people never develop.

Then, when the structure of the sport fades, the long-term planning muscle is suddenly expected to turn on without guidance. Income starts flowing. Decisions pile up. There is no judge's table. No posted score. No coach reviewing film.

Just outcomes that show up years later.

Money mistakes rarely look dramatic in the moment. They look small, manageable, and temporary. But like tiny form breaks, they compound over time. A missed savings habit here. A little lifestyle creep there. A few emotional decisions under pressure.

Eventually, the landing matters.

## *The Lie of Perfect Scores*

Gymnastics teaches you early that perfection is rare.

Even world-class athletes have deductions. Even gold medal routines are not flawless. What separates the best is not the absence of mistakes. It is the ability to manage them without losing control.

Money culture sells a different lie.

It tells people that if they just make the right move, everything will fall into place. Pick the right career. Buy the right asset. Invest in the right opportunity. That is the financial version of believing one perfect skill guarantees a perfect routine.

It does not.

Strong financial lives are built the same way strong gymnastics careers are built.

On fundamentals.

On consistency.

On knowing when to add difficulty and when to stay clean.

On respecting endurance, not just explosiveness.

Perfect scores are rare.

Sticking the landing is repeatable.

## *Why This Book Exists*

Gymnastics Money 101 exists because gymnasts already understand how hard things actually work.

You know that results come from reps.

You know that shortcuts show up on the scoreboard.

You know that pressure exposes weak fundamentals.

You know that finishes are trained, not improvised.

Yet almost none of that language is used when athletes are taught about money. Instead, financial education is either overly technical or insultingly simple. It rarely respects the intelligence and discipline athletes already bring to the table.

This book assumes you do not need motivation.

You need translation.

It translates money into a system you already understand.

Balance becomes budgeting.

Difficulty becomes risk.

Execution becomes discipline.

Falls become financial mistakes.

The landing becomes long-term stability.

The goal is not to turn you into a finance expert. The goal is to give you a routine that holds up when life adds pressure.

### *The Danger of Early Success Without Structure*

Some gymnasts experience early financial success.

Scholarships.

Coaching income.

Brand deals.

Entrepreneurial opportunities.

Career acceleration.

Early success feels like validation. It can also mask problems. When money is coming in, bad habits hide easily. Just like raw talent can hide poor form for a while.

Eventually, the difficulty increases.

Life adds complexity.

Responsibilities multiply.

Income becomes less predictable.

Time horizons get longer.

That is when structure matters most.

Many financially successful people fall not because they lack opportunity, but because they never built a system. They relied on talent, momentum, or confidence instead of fundamentals. When conditions changed, they had nothing to fall back on.

Gymnastics already taught you that lesson.

You do not rely on adrenaline in the final pass.

You rely on training.

### *Clean Routines Beat Flashy Ones*

Judges reward difficulty, but only when it is executed well.

The same is true financially.

You do not need complex strategies.

You do not need exclusive investments.

You do not need constant action.

You need clean execution.

A budget you actually follow beats a perfect plan you abandon.

Consistent saving beats sporadic big deposits.

Long-term investing beats chasing hot opportunities.

Protection beats hoping nothing goes wrong.

Clean routines finish strong.

Flashy routines fall apart under fatigue.

### *Why the End Matters More Than the Start*

Most people start strong financially.

They graduate motivated.

They get their first job excited.

They set goals.

They feel disciplined.

Then life happens.

Schedules disappear.

Accountability fades.

Comfort creeps in.

Decisions become reactive instead of intentional.

The end of the routine is where endurance shows up.

That is why this book spends so much time on structure, systems, and mindset. Not because the beginning does not matter, but because the end determines everything.

Nobody remembers a routine that started strong and fell apart.

Nobody remembers a financial life that looked good early and collapsed later.

What people respect is control.

What lasts is consistency.

What matters is sticking the landing.

## *A New Definition of Winning*

Gymnastics defines winning clearly when you are competing.

Scores.

Placements.

Podiums.

Money does not give you that clarity.

Winning financially is quieter.

It looks boring.

It shows up slowly.

It looks like optionality.

It looks like calm decisions under pressure.

It looks like flexibility instead of panic.

It looks like being able to say no.

It looks like finishing strong.

This book will help you build that version of winning.

Not the loud one.

The durable one.

## *What to Expect Moving Forward*

As you move through Gymnastics Money 101, you will see familiar patterns.

Preparation before performance.

Systems before difficulty.

Protection before growth.

Execution before emotion.

You will also see something gymnasts rarely get in financial conversations.

Permission to stop chasing perfection.

You do not need a perfect routine.

You need a routine you can repeat.

You do not need perfect timing.

You need consistency over time.

You do not need to impress anyone.

You need to protect yourself and your future.

Money is not scored after one meet.

It is scored after a lifetime.

## *The Point of the Routine*

The point of gymnastics was never just the score.

It was about mastery.

About control.

About becoming someone who could handle pressure.

Money is simply another arena where those traits matter.

This book is not asking you to become someone new.

It is asking you to apply what you already know.

Train the basics.

Respect the process.

Finish strong.

Perfect scores are rare.

Sticking the landing is the goal.

# About This Book

Gymnastics is one of the most honest sports in the world.

There is nowhere to hide. No teammate to bail you out. No clock to run. Every skill is judged on execution, control, and consistency. You either hit the routine, or you do not. The scoreboard does not care how hard the skill was supposed to be or how confident you felt before you saluted.

Money works the same way.

Outcomes matter more than intentions. Discipline matters more than talent. Consistency matters more than intensity. And just like gymnastics, the results often show up long after the training happened.

This book exists because gymnasts already understand the hardest parts of money. You just have not been shown how to translate them.

## *Gymnastics Is a System, Not a Moment*

From the outside, gymnastics looks like a collection of big skills.

Tumbling passes.

Release moves.

Dismounts.

Stuck landings.

But every gymnast knows that those moments sit on top of a system.

Warm-ups.

Basics.

Conditioning.

Reps.

Progressions.

Recovery.

Mental preparation.

No one walks into the gym and throws the hardest skill first. You build capacity before difficulty. You earn upgrades. You repeat fundamentals until they hold up under fatigue and pressure.

Money works exactly the same way.

People see the visible outcomes:

A house.

An investment account.

A business.

A lifestyle.

They rarely see the system underneath:

Budgeting.

Saving.

Risk management.

Patience.

Boring, repeatable habits.

Gymnastics teaches you that systems beat moments. This book applies that truth to money.

## *Balance Is Not Optional*

Gymnastics revolves around balance.

Not just on the beam, but everywhere.

Strength and flexibility.

Power and control.

Aggression and precision.

Difficulty and execution.

Too much of one without the other leads to deductions or injuries. You cannot muscle every skill. You cannot play it safe forever. You have to manage trade-offs constantly.

Money is built on the same balance.

Spending and saving.

Risk and protection.

Enjoying today and preparing for tomorrow.

Confidence and caution.

This book does not push extremes. It does not tell you to save everything or invest aggressively at all costs. It teaches balance because balance is what lasts.

A routine that looks impressive but wobbles constantly will not hold up.

A financial life built on extremes will not either.

## *Difficulty Adds Value Only When Executed Well*

In gymnastics, difficulty raises your potential score. It also raises your risk.

A harder routine only helps if you can execute it consistently. Otherwise, the deductions erase the benefit. Coaches know this. That is why upgrades are earned slowly and deliberately.

Financial decisions follow the same rule.

Higher risk investments can offer higher returns.

Complex strategies can add opportunity.

Leverage can amplify outcomes.

But only when the foundation is solid.

This book emphasizes fundamentals before complexity. It teaches you when to increase difficulty and when to stay clean. It reminds you that a simpler routine executed well beats a risky routine that falls apart under pressure.

Difficulty is optional.

Execution is not.

## *Reps Matter More Than Motivation*

Gymnastics does not rely on motivation.

You do not show up to practice only when you feel inspired. You show up because reps matter. Progress comes from repetition, not emotion.

Money is no different.

Waiting to feel motivated to save.

Waiting for the perfect time to invest.

Waiting until things feel easier.

Those are emotional decisions. They fail under pressure.

This book teaches you to build systems that run without motivation. Automated savings. Simple rules. Clear priorities. Just like practice schedules, these systems remove decision fatigue and keep you moving forward even when life gets busy.

Reps compound.

Habits compound.

Time compounds.

That is the real edge.

## *Judges, Scores, and Delayed Feedback*

One of the hardest parts of money is that feedback is delayed.

In gymnastics, you salute, perform, and get a score. You know quickly what worked and what did not.

Financial decisions do not work that way.

You can make a bad decision today and feel fine for years.

You can make a good decision today and feel uncomfortable in the short term.

The consequences often show up long after the choice.

Gymnasts are uniquely equipped for this challenge.

You already understand delayed payoff.

You already understand training without immediate reward.

You already understand trusting the process when results lag.

This book helps you apply that patience to money, where delayed feedback is the norm, not the exception.

## *Control Under Pressure*

Gymnastics is pressure training.

Crowds.

Judges.

Expectations.

One chance.

You are taught to breathe, focus, and execute when everything feels loud. You learn that panic causes mistakes and that rushing rarely helps.

Money creates pressure in different ways.

Unexpected expenses.

Market swings.

Career changes.

Social comparison.

Fear of falling behind.

The athletes who struggle financially are often not reckless. They are reactive. They let pressure dictate decisions. This book teaches you how to slow down, assess the situation, and respond instead of react.

Staying composed financially is the same skill as staying composed on the beam.

## *Why Analogies Matter*

This book uses gymnastics analogies because analogies are how learning sticks.

You do not need abstract theory. You need concepts tied to experience. When money is framed in familiar language, it stops feeling foreign and starts feeling manageable.

Budgeting becomes balance.

Risk becomes difficulty.

Diversification becomes routine composition.

Insurance becomes safety mats.

Emergency funds become spotters.

Rebalancing becomes mid-routine adjustments.

Retirement becomes sticking the landing.

These are not gimmicks. They are translations.

The goal is not to oversimplify money. The goal is to make it usable.

## *This Is Not About Perfection*

Gymnastics teaches perfectionism. Money punishes it.

Perfection leads to hesitation.

Hesitation leads to inaction.

Inaction leads to missed opportunity.

This book pushes progress over perfection.

You do not need a perfect budget.

You need a workable one.

You do not need the best investment strategy.

You need one you can stick with.

You do not need to eliminate mistakes.

You need to avoid catastrophic ones.

Clean execution beats flawless theory.

## *From Competition to Lifetime Performance*

Gymnastics careers are short.

Financial lives are long.

This book is designed to help you transition from competition thinking to lifetime performance thinking. Not one meet. Not one season. Not one big decision.

A career.

A life.

A finish that holds up.

Everything in Gymnastics Money 101 is built around that idea. Strong basics. Smart difficulty. Controlled execution. Protection against falls. And a focus on finishing well.

### *The Core Lesson*

Gymnastics already taught you the truth about success.

You earn it.

You train for it.

You respect the process.

You finish strong.

Money is not different.

It is just quieter.

This book exists to help you apply what you already know to a new arena. If you treat money like a routine instead of a gamble, you give yourself something most people never build.

Control.

Confidence.

And the ability to stick the landing.

# Foolish Assumptions

Every good coach starts with assumptions.

Not excuses. Not shortcuts. Assumptions about effort, accountability, and baseline competence. Coaches do not explain why showing up matters. They assume you will. They do not debate whether fundamentals matter. They build everything on them.

This section does the same thing.

These are the "foolish assumptions" this book makes about you. Foolish not because they are unrealistic, but because many books avoid saying them out loud. Gymnastics Money 101 assumes you are capable of more than you may currently believe, and it refuses to lower the standard.

## *Assumption 1: You Are Willing to Do the Basics, Even When They Are Boring*

Gymnastics is built on boring work.

Hollow holds.

Basics on low beam.

Hundreds of casts.

Endless drills that never make highlight reels.

This book assumes you understand that boring work wins.

Financial fundamentals are boring too.

Budgeting.

Saving.

Reviewing statements.

Staying consistent when nothing feels exciting.

If you are looking for hacks, shortcuts, or tricks, this is the wrong book. If you are willing to master the basics and repeat them long enough for results to compound, you are in the right place.

### *Assumption 2: You Respect Structure More Than Motivation*

Gymnastics does not run on motivation.

You train on days you feel great and days you do not. You follow the plan even when energy is low. You understand that discipline carries you when motivation disappears.

This book assumes you respect structure.

You do not need to feel inspired to manage money.

You need systems that run whether you feel inspired or not.

Automated savings.

Clear rules.

Simple routines.

If you believe motivation should drive behavior, money will feel inconsistent. If you believe structure drives results, money becomes manageable.

### *Assumption 3: You Can Handle Honest Feedback*

Gymnastics is honest.

The mirror is honest.

The video is honest.

The judge is honest.

This book assumes you can handle the truth about your finances without shutting down, getting defensive, or avoiding the numbers.

You may discover:

You spend more than you thought.

You saved less than you assumed.

You avoided decisions instead of making them.

That is not failure. That is film study.

Improvement starts with honesty. This book assumes you are mature enough to face it.

## *Assumption 4: You Understand That Perfection Is Not the Goal*

Gymnastics rewards precision, but perfectionism destroys progress.

Waiting until everything is perfect leads to hesitation.

Hesitation leads to missed reps.

Missed reps lead to stagnation.

This book assumes you are willing to act imperfectly.

You will not have the perfect budget.

You will not time investments perfectly.

You will make mistakes.

Progress comes from clean execution over time, not flawless planning. If you are waiting to feel "ready," you will wait too long.

## *Assumption 5: You Are Coachable Outside the Gym*

Some athletes struggle after sport because they stop being coachable.

They take feedback personally.

They assume past success guarantees future success.

They resist learning from people who were not part of their athletic journey.

This book assumes you are still coachable.

Money is a new event. Being elite in gymnastics does not automatically translate to elite financial decision-making. That is not a flaw. It is reality.

If you can listen, learn, and apply new skills, you will progress quickly.

### *Assumption 6: You Care About Finishing Strong, Not Just Starting Fast*

Gymnastics careers end early.

Financial lives do not.

This book assumes you care more about long-term stability than short-term appearances. More about sticking the landing than flashing difficulty early.

That means:

You value sustainability over hype.

You protect downside as much as you chase upside.

You understand that a clean routine beats a risky one that falls apart.

If your goal is to look successful instead of being secure, money will stay stressful. This book assumes you want real control, not optics.

### *Assumption 7: You Are Willing to Take Responsibility*

Gymnastics teaches personal responsibility early.

If you miss a skill, you own it.

If you fall, you reset.

If you fail, you go back to basics.

This book assumes you accept responsibility for your financial decisions.

Not blame.

Not shame.

Responsibility.

That means:

You do not outsource decisions blindly.

You do not rely on luck.

You do not avoid learning because it feels uncomfortable.

You own your outcomes.

### *Assumption 8: You Understand That Pressure Reveals Systems*

In competition, pressure reveals preparation.

When nerves hit, you do not rise to the occasion. You fall back to your training.

Money works the same way.

Under stress, you will not make better decisions.

You will make familiar ones.

This book assumes you want systems that hold up when pressure shows up. Systems that keep you steady during market drops, income changes, and unexpected life events.

### *Assumption 9: You Are Not Afraid of Long-Term Thinking*

Gymnastics rewards patience.

Skills take months or years to develop.

Strength builds slowly.

Confidence grows through repetition.

This book assumes you are comfortable thinking in seasons, not moments.

Money rewards:

Consistency.

Time.

Delayed gratification.

If you are chasing fast wins, you will take unnecessary risk. If you are willing to stack good days for years, you will build something durable.

### *Assumption 10: You Want Control, Not Just Knowledge*

Information alone does not change outcomes.

Gymnasts know this.

Watching a skill does not mean you can perform it.

Understanding a drill does not mean you have mastered it.

This book assumes you want control over your money, not just information about it.

Control comes from:

Habits.

Systems.

Repetition.

Accountability.

That is what this book is designed to build.

### *The Bottom Line*

These assumptions are not meant to exclude you. They are meant to challenge you.

Gymnastics already taught you:

Effort is non-negotiable.

Details matter.

Consistency beats intensity.

You do not cheat the work.

This book assumes you are ready to apply those lessons to money.

If you are, everything that follows will make sense.

If you are not, nothing will stick.

The choice is the same as it always was.

Commit to the process, or keep starting over.

# How This Routine Is Organized

Gymnastics routines are not random.

Every routine is built with intention. Skills are placed in a specific order. Strength elements set up flight elements. Transitions matter. The goal is not to cram in difficulty, but to move cleanly from start to finish while staying in control. A routine that looks impressive early but unravels at the end does not win.

This book is organized the same way.

**Gymnastics Money 101** is not meant to be read like a reference manual or skimmed for quick tips. It is designed like a well-constructed routine. Each section builds on the one before it. Skipping fundamentals makes later sections harder to execute. Mastering the basics makes everything else feel lighter and more natural.

Here is how the routine flows.

## *The Front Matter: Setting the Tone*

The foreword and introduction establish one core truth:

Perfect scores do not matter if you fall at the end.

Many athletes work incredibly hard, earn money, and look successful on the surface, only to struggle later because fundamentals were ignored early. The opening pages explain why this book exists, who it is for, and why gymnastics provides such a powerful framework for understanding money.

This section is about mindset, not mechanics. It prepares you to approach money the same way you approached training: with patience, structure, and respect for fundamentals.

### *Part I: Building the Base (Foundations and Form)*

Every routine starts with basics.

Before big skills come balance, posture, strength, and control. In gymnastics, weak basics show up later under pressure. In money, the same thing happens.

Part I focuses on the financial equivalents of form and fundamentals:

- Understanding why money feels overwhelming after sport
- Getting clear on income, expenses, and cash flow
- Learning how budgeting and saving actually work in real life
- Understanding credit, debt, and deductions
- Setting up clean, functional banking systems

This section is intentionally unglamorous.

That is the point.

If you rush through this part, later chapters will feel stressful and confusing. If you master it, everything else becomes easier. Just like gymnastics, strong basics make advanced skills feel controlled instead of chaotic.

### *Part II: Stability and Protection*

Once form is solid, gymnasts focus on control and safety.

You do not add difficulty if you cannot stay on the apparatus. You learn how to fall safely. You build awareness of risk. You protect yourself so you can keep training.

Part II applies that same logic to money through:

- Risk awareness and decision-making
- Insurance fundamentals
- Life, disability, and liability protection

This section is about staying in the routine.

Unexpected events derail people financially not because they are careless, but because they are unprotected. This part of the book helps you understand how to manage risk without becoming fearful or overly conservative.

Stability allows confidence. Confidence allows progress.

## *Part III: Building Difficulty and Value (Investing Fundamentals)*

Difficulty adds value only when executed cleanly.

In gymnastics, difficulty without control leads to falls. In money, investing without understanding leads to panic, poor timing, and long-term damage.

Part III introduces investing step by step:

- How markets actually work
- The relationship between risk, return, and compounding
- What owning stocks really means
- How bonds create balance
- How funds and ETFs simplify investing
- When real estate and alternatives fit, and when they do not

This section is designed to remove mystery, not create excitement.

You are not being trained to chase hot investments. You are learning how ownership works, how value is created over time, and why patience matters more than predictions.

## *Part IV: Managing the Routine (Execution and Adjustments)*

Great gymnasts adjust without losing form.

They know when to push, when to stay clean, and when to reset. They review film. They make small corrections instead of emotional overhauls.

Part IV focuses on execution:

- Asset allocation and portfolio structure
- Opening and managing investment accounts

- Buy-and-hold discipline
- Rebalancing and making adjustments
- The mental side of money and pressure

This section teaches you how to stay composed once real money is involved. Markets move. Life changes. Emotions show up. Systems are what keep you steady.

The goal here is not perfection. It is consistency under pressure.

## *Part V: The Long Career and Sticking the Landing*

In gymnastics, how you finish matters.

Fatigue sets in late. Focus wavers. Small mistakes appear. Championships are often decided in the final moments of a routine.

Part V looks at the long view:

- Taxes and where your score really shows up
- Retirement accounts and long-term independence
- Housing and major financial decisions
- Career income, benefits, and negotiation
- Estate planning basics
- Family conversations about money

This is where many athletes struggle, not because they lack ability, but because no one taught them how to plan beyond competition.

This section is about translating discipline into decades, not seasons.

## *Part VI: Long-Term Success*

The final section is about sustainability.

It covers:

- When and how to use advisors

- How to recognize scams and bad advice
- Common financial mistakes athletes make
- Clear rules for long-term success

This part reinforces that you do not need to do everything alone, but you do need to stay engaged and informed.

Strong routines are not solo efforts. Neither are strong financial lives.

### *Back Matter: Tools for the Future*

The glossary, resources, disclaimers, and index are included so you can revisit concepts, clarify terms, and continue learning long after the final page.

This book is not meant to be read once and forgotten. Like training notes or old routines, it is something you return to as your life changes.

### *How to Use This Book*

You can read this book cover to cover, or you can revisit sections as needed. However, the structure matters.

If money feels overwhelming, start at the beginning.

If investing feels intimidating, check your foundations first.

If stress is showing up, look at protection and systems.

Just like gymnastics, progress comes from respecting the order.

### *One Final Reminder About Structure*

Gymnastics taught you this already:

- Basics before difficulty
- Control before risk
- Consistency before confidence
- Finish matters

This book is organized to follow that same truth.

If you trust the structure, execute the reps, and stay patient, the routine holds together.

And when pressure shows up, you will be ready to stick the landing.

# About Pat Brown

Pat Brown played college football at the University of Kansas from 1994 to 1999 and was named team captain for the 1999 season. His years in the locker room shaped his views on accountability, discipline, preparation, and leadership. Those principles continue to guide his work long after football.

Following his playing career, Pat transitioned into financial services and built a career as a financial advisor and wealth manager. He works with individuals, families, business owners, and athletes who are navigating increasingly complex financial lives. His work focuses on helping people make clear, disciplined decisions around money rather than reacting emotionally or chasing shortcuts.

Pat pursued advanced education and professional development to match real-world experience with technical expertise. He earned his MBA and holds multiple advanced financial designations, including ChFC®, RICP®, and CAP®. His background spans comprehensive financial planning, retirement income strategies, tax-aware decision making, and philanthropy. More importantly, it reflects a commitment to doing the work the right way, not the easy way.

As the college sports landscape changed with the introduction of Name, Image, and Likeness opportunities, Pat recognized a growing education gap. Student-athletes were gaining access to income, contracts, and endorsements without the financial knowledge needed to manage taxes, cash flow, business structures, and long-term consequences. Many were being asked to perform at a high level financially without ever being taught the fundamentals.

That reality became the catalyst for Pat's work in athlete financial education.

He has since become a recognized voice in this space and has been interviewed by national publications and platforms including Financial Planning, Yahoo, and ESPN Andscape. In those conversations, Pat focuses on practical realities rather than headlines, emphasizing structure, preparation, and decision-making under pressure.

These experiences led Pat to author a series of athlete-focused books designed to meet athletes and families where they are. His NIL-related titles include *Financial Literacy for NIL, Financial Literacy for NIL for Parents of Student-Athletes, Financial Literacy for NIL for High School Students,* and *Financial Literacy for NIL for International Student-Athletes.* Each book is written to be clear, accessible, and grounded in real-world scenarios rather than theory.

Pat also created a growing collection of sport-specific financial education titles, including *Football Money 101, Baseball Money 101, Basketball Money 101, Cheer Money 101, Dance Money 101, Gymnastics Money 101, Hockey Money 101, Lacrosse Money 101, Rowing Money 101, Soccer Money 101, Softball Money 101, Tennis Money 101, Track Money 101, Volleyball Money 101,* and *Wrestling Money 101.* Each book translates the culture, discipline, and mindset of a specific sport into financial lessons athletes can apply long after competition ends.

To extend this mission beyond books, Pat founded **Former Student Athlete**, a platform built to support athletes navigating life after sports. The platform provides education, community, and real-world resources focused on financial literacy, career transitions, health, identity, and long-term success once the uniform comes off. His work can be explored at:

- www.formerstudentathlete.com
- www.financialliteracyfornil.com
- www.financialliteracyforstudentathletes.com

Pat is easy to find through a Google search, on LinkedIn, or on Twitter, where he regularly shares insights on athletes, money, and life after sports. If you would like to connect with Pat specifically about **Gymnastics Money**

**101**, you can reach him directly at:

**info@gymnasticsmoney101.com**

Pat's work is rooted in a belief shaped by both athletics and finance. Athletes deserve a better playbook for life after sports, and financial education should arrive before opportunity turns into regret.

# Part I: Building the Base (Foundations and Form)

Every routine starts with strong basics.

In gymnastics, nothing matters if the foundation is weak. You can have difficulty, power, and flexibility, but without form, balance, and control, the routine breaks down. Deductions add up quickly. Small errors early turn into bigger problems later. Even elite gymnasts know this truth. You do not skip basics. You master them.

Money works the same way.

Most financial stress does not come from complex investing mistakes. It comes from weak fundamentals. No structure. No system. No awareness of where money is going or why decisions are being made. When the base is unstable, everything built on top of it feels shaky.

This section is about foundations.

Before difficulty is added, before growth is chased, before long-term goals are mapped out, the basics have to be solid. That means understanding cash flow, building simple systems, learning how credit works, and setting up accounts that support good habits instead of fighting them.

These chapters are not flashy. They are not exciting. They are essential.

In gymnastics, basics are trained daily. Handstands. Hollow body positions. Landings. They are repeated so often they become automatic. Financial basics deserve the same repetition. When systems are simple and habits are consistent, decisions get easier. Stress goes down. Confidence goes up.

Part I is about form.

It is about learning how to stay balanced before you try to add difficulty. It is about building routines that hold under pressure. It is about giving yourself a base strong enough to support everything that comes next.

You do not need perfection here. You need consistency.

Get the basics right, and the rest of the routine has a chance to shine.

# Chapter 1: Why Money Feels Overwhelming After Gymnastics

Think back to your first real competition.

Not an in-house meet. Not a controlled environment. A real meet, with judges, lights, noise, and pressure. The equipment felt the same. The skills were the same ones you trained every day. But everything felt faster. Tighter. Less forgiving.

Small balance checks mattered.

Tiny form breaks showed up.

One missed connection affected the entire routine.

It was not because you were unprepared. It was because competition changes how information shows up.

Money works the same way.

Most gymnasts do not struggle with money because they are careless or irresponsible. They struggle because they leave a highly structured, coached environment and suddenly face real financial decisions without a routine, without reps, and without feedback.

One day, gymnastics controls nearly every hour of your life. Training schedules. Meet calendars. Nutrition plans. Travel. Recovery. Then the final salute happens, and you are expected to manage income, expenses, credit, taxes, and long-term decisions on your own.

No walkthrough.

No compulsory routine.

No coach correcting form mid-set.

That is why money feels overwhelming.

## *Why Financial Literacy Is Rarely Taught to Athletes*

Gymnasts grow up in structured systems by design.

Practice times are set.

Skills progressions are planned.

Competitions are scheduled.

Coaches decide when difficulty is added.

Judges provide immediate feedback.

That structure allows you to focus on execution. It is not a flaw. It is the reason athletes improve.

The problem appears when the structure disappears.

Financial education is often treated as someone else's responsibility. Schools assume families will teach it. Families assume athletes will figure it out later. Programs focus on performance, not paychecks. Even when income starts showing up through coaching, judging, camps, or NIL opportunities, education rarely arrives first.

By the time money matters, the learning curve is already steep.

In gymnastics terms, it is like being asked to perform an optional routine without ever being taught the compulsory basics. The expectation is there, but the foundation is missing.

Money feels confusing not because you lack discipline, but because no one handed you a routine.

## *Money Myths Learned Early in Competition Culture*

Gymnastics culture quietly teaches beliefs about money, even when it does not intend to.

You learn that perfection matters.

You learn that mistakes are costly.

You learn that results define value.

You learn to compare scores constantly.

Those lessons make sense in competition. They become dangerous when applied to money.

Common myths show up early:

"If you are not investing aggressively, you are falling behind."

"More income automatically means success."

"Saving is for people who are scared."

"You need to find the perfect strategy."

"Everyone else seems to have it figured out."

These ideas spread the same way bad habits spread in the gym. One confident voice. One highlight story. One example taken out of context.

In gymnastics, you would never overhaul your routine because someone else hit a big skill once. With money, people do it all the time.

Money myths thrive because they are emotional, not because they are accurate.

## *Saving vs Investing vs Gambling*

This confusion causes more stress for athletes than almost anything else.

Saving, investing, and gambling are not the same thing.

Saving is about protection.

It is money you can access quickly.

Emergency funds.

Short-term needs.

Stability.

Investing is about ownership and growth over time.

You accept ups and downs.

You stay patient.

You let time and discipline do the work.

Gambling is chasing outcomes without a routine.

No protection.

No margin for error.

Emotion-driven decisions.

Hope instead of structure.

In gymnastics terms:

Saving is basics and conditioning.

It is not exciting, but it keeps you healthy and consistent.

Investing is building difficulty carefully over time.

Progressions.

Reps.

Trusting the process.

Gambling is throwing a big skill without preparation and hoping the judges reward it.

Many former gymnasts skip saving because it feels slow and unglamorous. They jump straight to investing or speculation. That is like skipping basics and expecting to hit difficulty consistently. It might work once. It eventually fails.

Strong routines always start with protection.

## *Why Consistency Beats Chasing Perfect Scores*

Gymnastics teaches a painful but valuable truth.

Perfect scores are rare.

Clean routines win more often than risky ones.

Consistency keeps you competitive.

Money follows the same rules.

You do not need the perfect budget.

You need a simple one you can follow.

You do not need the perfect investment strategy.

You need one you can stick with through good and bad seasons.

You do not need to master everything immediately.

You need to start and keep showing up.

Consistency builds confidence.

Confidence reduces emotional decisions.

Reduced emotion leads to better outcomes.

The athletes who struggle financially are often the same ones who chase perfection. They wait for the ideal plan. The ideal income level. The ideal moment. While they wait, nothing compounds.

In gymnastics, waiting to be perfect delays progress. In money, it does the same.

## *The Hidden Transition After Gymnastics*

One of the hardest adjustments after gymnastics is the loss of constant feedback.

Judges stop scoring.

Coaches stop correcting.

Practice schedules disappear.

Accountability becomes optional.

Money exposes this gap quickly.

Without a routine, habits fade.

Without structure, decisions become reactive.

Without feedback, mistakes repeat quietly.

That is why money mistakes often show up years later, not immediately. Just like form errors that cause injury over time, financial habits compound slowly before the damage becomes obvious.

This book exists to rebuild that structure.

## *Coach's Perspective: What Would Your Coach Say?*

A gymnastics coach would not overcomplicate this.

"Master the basics."

"Form before difficulty."

"Reps matter."

"Stay patient."

"Do not rush what you have not earned."

"Trust the process."

Those same rules apply to money.

You do not need to be perfect.

You do need to be consistent.

You do not need flash.

You need control.

Money rewards athletes who treat it like training, not competition.

## *Game Situations and Decision Points*

You start earning money for the first time.

Do you save something immediately, or wait until later?

You hear about a fast way to grow money.

Do you understand the risk, or just the upside?

You feel behind compared to others.

Do you force decisions, or build your base patiently?

In gymnastics, forcing skills leads to falls.

In money, forcing decisions leads to regret.

## *Common Athlete Mistakes and Financial Parallels*

Gymnasts chase perfect scores.

Financially, that leads to overcomplication.

Gymnasts compare routines constantly.

Financially, that leads to misaligned decisions.

Gymnasts skip basics once they feel advanced.

Financially, that leads to fragile systems.

The habits that build medals are the same habits that build stability. The context just changes.

## *Winning the Long Game*

Gymnastics careers are short.

Financial lives are long.

You do not need to win today.

You need to stay upright.

You need to finish routines.

You need to stick the landing.

Money feels overwhelming after gymnastics because the structure disappeared, not because you lost discipline. This book is here to help you rebuild a routine that works in the next phase of your life.

Form first.

Balance first.

Consistency first.

### *Athlete Takeaways*

- Basics come before difficulty. Always.
- Saving protects you. Investing grows you. Gambling guesses.
- Loud advice is not the same as good coaching.
- Clean, repeatable routines beat risky perfection.
- Stay patient, trust the reps, and build your base.

# Chapter 2: Check Your Scorecard – Your Financial Snapshot

Every gymnast knows this moment.

You finish your routine, salute the judges, and walk off the floor. You might feel great. You might feel frustrated. You might replay one wobble or one stuck landing in your head. But none of that determines the outcome.

The score does.

Difficulty. Execution. Deductions. Final number.

The scorecard does not care how hard the routine felt or how confident you were going in. It shows what actually happened.

Money has a scorecard too.

Most former gymnasts avoid it. Not because they are reckless or irresponsible, but because no one ever taught them how to read it. Bank balances feel disconnected. Bills hit at different times. Spending happens automatically. Income feels irregular. Instead of looking at the numbers, people rely on how things feel.

That is how small problems quietly turn into big ones.

Before you change anything, before you set goals, before you build a plan, you need to check the scorecard.

## *Income, Expenses, and Cash Flow*

Cash flow is how money moves through your life.

Income is what comes in.

Paychecks.

Coaching income.

Judging fees.

Bonuses.

Side work.

NIL income for some athletes.

Expenses are what go out.

Rent.

Food.

Transportation.

Insurance.

Subscriptions.

Lifestyle spending.

Cash flow is the difference.

In gymnastics terms, income is your difficulty score.

Expenses are your deductions.

Cash flow is the final score that actually matters.

A lot of gymnasts focus only on income. More money feels like progress. Just like adding difficulty feels like improvement. But if execution gets worse at the same time, the score does not improve.

More income with equally rising expenses does not move you forward.

Positive cash flow gives you options.

Negative cash flow puts you under pressure.

You do not need complex spreadsheets or fancy software to understand this. You need awareness.

What comes in.

What goes out.

What is left.

Everything else builds on that foundation.

## *Why Cash Flow Matters More Than Income Alone*

Gymnastics teaches you that difficulty without control is dangerous.

Money works the same way.

Two people can earn the same income and live completely different financial lives. One has flexibility. The other feels stressed and trapped. The difference is cash flow.

Positive cash flow allows you to:

Build savings.

Invest consistently.

Handle surprises.

Make decisions from strength.

Negative cash flow forces you to:

Use credit.

Delay goals.

React emotionally.

Feel constant pressure.

Just like routines, money systems either support you or fight you. Cash flow tells you which one you are running.

## *Assets, Liabilities, and Net Worth*

The next part of your financial scorecard is net worth.

Assets are things you own that have value.

Cash.

Savings.

Investments.

Retirement accounts.

Property.

Businesses.

Liabilities are what you owe.

Credit cards.

Student loans.

Car loans.

Personal loans.

Mortgages.

Net worth is the difference.

Assets minus liabilities.

In gymnastics terms, assets are your strengths.

Flexibility.

Power.

Consistency.

Experience.

Liabilities are your vulnerabilities.

Chronic injuries.

Form breaks.

Mental mistakes.

Net worth is the full routine score.

Not one skill.

Not one event.

The entire picture.

One big asset does not erase multiple weaknesses. Just like one strong event does not win a meet if the rest of the routine falls apart.

Many former gymnasts confuse income with wealth. Income is what you earn this month. Net worth is what you are building over time.

Income pays the bills.

Net worth creates stability.

## *Why Net Worth Feels Uncomfortable to Look At*

Net worth forces honesty.

It shows decisions made years ago.

It shows habits, not intentions.

It shows patterns, not excuses.

That is why people avoid it.

But avoiding the scorecard does not change the score. It just delays improvement.

In gymnastics, ignoring deductions does not make them disappear. Reviewing them is how you clean up routines.

Money works the same way.

Net worth is not a judgment. It is information. Information gives you control.

## *Fixed vs Variable Expenses*

Not all expenses are equal.

Fixed expenses stay mostly the same each month.

Rent or mortgage.

Insurance.

Loan payments.

Phone plans.

Gym memberships.

Variable expenses change.

Food.

Travel.

Entertainment.

Convenience spending.

Shopping.

Lifestyle choices.

In gymnastics terms, fixed expenses are your compulsory elements.

They define the structure of your routine.

Variable expenses are execution.

That is where adjustments happen.

Most people try to change big fixed costs first, which is often difficult and slow. The real leverage is usually in variable spending that goes unnoticed.

Small purchases.

Repeated habits.

Convenience decisions.

One coffee does not matter.

Twenty a week does.

Little deductions add up over a season.

### *Why Variable Expenses Matter More Than You Think*

Variable expenses are where habits live.

They reflect:

Stress.

Fatigue.

Reward patterns.

Impulse decisions.

Just like form breaks appear late in routines, variable spending often increases when discipline fades. End of long days. Emotional spending. Rewarding effort instead of results.

Tracking variable expenses is not about guilt. It is about awareness.

You cannot clean up what you cannot see.

### *Reviewing Where Your Money Actually Goes*

This is the hardest part for most athletes.

Pull your bank statements.

Pull your credit card statements.

Look at them honestly.

No judgment.

No shame.

No excuses.

This is film study.

Film study is not punishment.

It is preparation.

You might find:

Subscriptions you forgot about.

Spending that does not align with what you say matters.

Patterns tied to stress or boredom.

Expenses that quietly grew over time.

The goal is not to criticize past decisions. The goal is to understand them.

If you do not watch the film, you repeat the same mistakes.

## *Why Awareness Changes Behavior*

Once gymnasts see their routines on video, things change.

They notice habits they did not feel.

They clean up details.

They adjust proactively.

Money works the same way.

Awareness alone improves outcomes.

Not perfection.

Not restriction.

Awareness.

When you know your numbers, decisions become easier. You stop guessing. You stop reacting. You start choosing.

## *Coach's Perspective: What Would Your Coach Say?*

A coach would not let you guess how you performed.

"The scorecard doesn't lie."

"Look at the numbers."

"Fix the basics first."

"Details matter."

"You cannot improve what you refuse to see."

Avoiding the score does not protect you. Reviewing it gives you control.

## *Game Situations and Decision Points*

You feel like you are doing fine, but your account balance never grows.

Do you blame income, or review expenses?

You get a raise or new income stream.

Do you upgrade your lifestyle immediately, or improve cash flow first?
You have debt but no clear picture of totals.
Do you avoid it, or list it out and face it?
Just like gymnastics, progress starts with honest evaluation.

### *Common Athlete Mistakes and Financial Parallels*

Gymnasts rely on feel instead of film.
Financially, that means guessing instead of tracking.
Gymnasts avoid watching bad routines.
Financially, that means avoiding statements.
Gymnasts overvalue one strong event.
Financially, that means one good paycheck masking weak habits.
The patterns repeat.

### *Winning the Long Game*

Strong gymnasts know their scores, not just how routines feel.
Strong financial lives are built the same way.
Your financial snapshot is not about judgment.
It is about clarity.
Clarity leads to control.
Control leads to confidence.
This is how you stop feeling behind.
This is how you build a routine that holds up under pressure.

### *Athlete Takeaways*

- Check the scorecard before changing the routine.
- Income means nothing without positive cash flow.
- Assets build stability. Liabilities create pressure.
- Fixed expenses set structure. Variable expenses reveal habits.
- Watch the film. Awareness is the first rep toward improvement.

# Chapter 3: Mastering Balance – Budgeting and Saving

Every gymnast learns this early.

Balance is not optional.

You can have incredible strength, flexibility, and difficulty, but if you cannot stay centered, the routine falls apart. A beam routine does not fail because the gymnast is weak. It fails because balance breaks under pressure. A tiny lean turns into a wobble. A wobble turns into a step. A step turns into a fall.

Money works the same way.

Most financial problems are not caused by lack of income or effort. They come from imbalance. Spending that leans too far one way. Saving that gets skipped when things feel tight. Decisions made without a stable center.

Budgeting and saving are how you build financial balance. Not perfection. Not restriction. Balance.

## *Budgeting Systems That Actually Work*

A budget is not punishment.

It is not about cutting everything fun.

It is not about tracking every dollar obsessively.

It is not about guilt.

A budget is balance.

In gymnastics terms, a budget is knowing where your weight is supposed to be throughout the routine. It keeps you centered so small shifts do not throw you off.

Most budgets fail because they are built like impossible routines. Too complex. Too strict. Too disconnected from real life. Gymnasts do not train routines they cannot hit consistently. Money systems should work the same way.

Effective budgeting systems share a few traits:

They are simple.

They are realistic.

They are repeatable.

At its core, budgeting answers three questions:

How much money comes in?

What expenses must be covered?

What is left to direct intentionally?

That is it.

You do not need to label every dollar with perfection. You need awareness and structure. When money has an assignment, it behaves better. When it does not, it wanders.

In gymnastics, uncontrolled movement creates deductions. In money, uncontrolled spending does the same.

## *Why Budgeting Feels Hard After Gymnastics*

Gymnastics provides structure automatically.

Practice times.

Conditioning blocks.

Recovery schedules.

Competition calendars.

After gymnastics, that structure disappears. No one sets your schedule. No one checks your habits. No one corrects small mistakes early.

Without structure, discipline becomes optional.

Budgeting replaces the structure you lost. It becomes your personal routine. Without it, every expense feels like a balance check you did not prepare for.

## *Automating Savings Like Daily Practice*

Gymnasts do not debate whether to do basics.

You do handstands.

You do turns.

You do shaping drills.

Not because they are exciting, but because they are necessary.

Saving should work the same way.

If you wait to save whatever is left at the end of the month, you will rarely save anything. Life fills the space. Unexpected expenses show up. Convenience wins. Discipline fades.

Automation fixes this.

Direct deposit into savings.

Automatic transfers.

Scheduled contributions.

In gymnastics terms, this is daily basics. You do not rely on motivation. You rely on routine.

Automation removes emotion from the equation. Emotion is where financial mistakes live. When saving happens automatically, progress happens quietly in the background.

You may not feel it at first. Just like strength gains. Then one day, you realize you are more stable than you used to be.

## *Why Saving First Changes Everything*

Saving first does two powerful things.

It protects you.

It builds confidence.

When saving happens before spending, you stop hoping things work out. You know you are making progress. That confidence reduces stress, which improves decision-making everywhere else.

In gymnastics, confidence comes from knowing you trained the basics. Financial confidence comes from knowing you protected yourself first.

## *Emergency Funds as Injury Protection*

Every gymnast understands injury risk.

You do not plan to get hurt.

You prepare anyway.

Ice baths.

Physical therapy.

Prehab.

Recovery days.

An emergency fund is the financial version of that mindset.

It is cash set aside for the unexpected.

Medical bills.

Car repairs.

Job changes.

Delayed paychecks.

Life disruptions.

Without an emergency fund, every surprise becomes a crisis. You reach for credit. You panic. You abandon the plan.

With an emergency fund, you stay composed. You handle the situation and continue training.

That is staying in the routine.

## *How Big Should an Emergency Fund Be?*

There is no perfect number.

The goal is not perfection.

The goal is protection.

Start small if needed.

Build consistently.

Increase over time.

In gymnastics terms, you do not start on the high beam without mastering low beam. You progress.

An emergency fund is not an investment. It is insurance. It is there so you do not fall when something unexpected happens.

## *Balancing Lifestyle With Long-Term Goals*

This is where many former gymnasts struggle.

You trained hard.

You sacrificed.

You delayed fun.

You feel like you deserve to enjoy life.

That feeling is valid.

The mistake is turning short-term comfort into long-term imbalance.

Gymnastics teaches delayed gratification. You train for months for a few minutes of competition. Money requires the same mindset. Enjoying life today should not come at the cost of limiting your future.

Balance does not mean deprivation.

It means:

Spending intentionally.

Saving consistently.

Aligning money with what actually matters.

In gymnastics, every movement serves a purpose. Financially, spending should do the same.

## *Why Lifestyle Creep Breaks Balance*

Lifestyle creep is subtle.

Income increases.

Spending quietly follows.

Saving stays the same.

Nothing feels wrong in the moment. Over time, pressure builds.

In gymnastics terms, this is slowly leaning forward on beam. One step does not matter. Over time, balance disappears.

Budgeting and saving keep lifestyle choices intentional instead of reactive.

## *Coach's Perspective: What Would Your Coach Say?*

A coach would not overcomplicate this.

"Stay centered."

"Control your body."

"Do the basics."

"Details matter."

"Finish the routine."

Budgeting and saving are boring for the same reason basics are boring. They work.

No coach builds a routine without balance. No financial plan works without it either.

## *Game Situations and Decision Points*

You get paid.

Do you save first, or hope there is something left?

You want to upgrade your lifestyle.

Do you check your balance, or react emotionally?

An unexpected expense shows up.

Do you stay composed, or reach for credit?

These moments are balance checks. Preparation determines the outcome.

## *Common Athlete Mistakes and Financial Parallels*

Gymnasts skip basics.

Financially, that means skipping savings.

Gymnasts rush difficulty.

Financially, that means spending before stability.

Gymnasts ignore small wobbles.

Financially, that means letting habits slide.

The same mistakes repeat in different forms.

### *Winning the Long Game*

Balanced routines finish strong.

Balanced financial lives do too.

Budgeting and saving are not about control. They are about freedom. Freedom to make choices. Freedom to handle setbacks. Freedom to stay upright when pressure hits.

This is how you stop falling late in the routine.

### *Athlete Takeaways*

- A budget is balance, not restriction.
- Automate savings like daily basics.
- Emergency funds protect you when life hits unexpectedly.
- Lifestyle choices should support long-term stability.
- Master balance first, then build difficulty.

# Chapter 4: Credit, Debt, and Avoiding Deductions

Every gymnast understands deductions.

You can train for years.

You can hit most of the routine.

You can show strength, flexibility, and control.

And still lose the meet because of small mistakes.

A step on the landing.

A balance check.

A form break.

A hesitation.

Individually, they do not feel catastrophic. Together, they add up. Judges do not care how hard the routine was supposed to be. They score what actually happened.

Credit and debt work the same way.

Most people do not experience one dramatic financial failure. They lose points slowly. Late payments here. High balances there. Convenience decisions that feel harmless in the moment. Over time, those deductions compound and limit options.

Credit is not about being perfect.

It is about avoiding unnecessary deductions.

## *How Credit Scores and Reports Work*

Your credit score is not a judgment of your character.

It is a scoring system.

Just like gymnastics, it evaluates execution, not intention.

A credit score measures how you handle borrowed money based on a few key factors:

Do you pay on time?

How much of your available credit do you use?

How long have you been using credit?

How often do you apply for new credit?

What types of credit do you use?

In gymnastics terms, this is consistency of execution. You do not get extra credit for trying hard. You get credit for hitting the routine cleanly.

Your credit report is the score sheet.

Your credit score is the final number.

You cannot argue with it.

You cannot explain your intentions.

You can only improve it through behavior.

This is good news. It means credit is controllable.

## *Why Credit Matters More Than You Think*

Credit affects far more than loans.

It impacts:

Interest rates on cars and homes.

Insurance premiums in some cases.

Rental applications.

Job background checks.

Access to opportunities.

In gymnastics terms, credit is reputation. When judges trust your execution, they score you fairly. When trust is broken, scrutiny increases.

Good credit does not guarantee success.

Poor credit quietly closes doors.

## *Credit Cards, Loans, and Interest*

Credit cards and loans are tools.

They are not good or bad by default. Their impact depends on how they are used.

Interest is the cost of borrowing.

It is the deduction applied every month you carry a balance.

The longer the balance remains, the more points you lose.

In gymnastics terms, interest is like performing with bent knees or flexed feet. It may not end the routine immediately, but it bleeds points relentlessly.

Credit cards are often the most dangerous because they feel harmless. Small balances. Easy payments. Flexible minimums. That flexibility creates false confidence.

Loans feel more structured. Fixed payments. Clear timelines. But they still require discipline.

Borrowed money always comes with expectations.

## *Why Interest Is So Dangerous Over Time*

Interest compounds against you.

That means you are paying interest on interest, not just on what you borrowed.

In gymnastics terms, this is letting deductions stack. One mistake creates another. Recovery becomes harder the longer you wait.

Many athletes assume they will "fix it later" when income improves. Sometimes that works. Often, the damage is already done.

Discipline early prevents stress later.

## *Good Debt vs Bad Debt*

Not all debt is the same.

Good debt helps you build something that improves your future options.

Education that increases earning potential.

A reasonably priced home.

Business investments with a plan.

Bad debt finances consumption.

Lifestyle upgrades.

Status purchases.

Impulse spending that fades quickly but leaves long-term payments.

In gymnastics terms, good debt is investing in basics and conditioning. Bad debt is chasing difficulty before form is solid.

The difference is not the interest rate alone.

The difference is whether the debt creates future stability or future pressure.

## *Why Athletes Are Vulnerable to Debt Mistakes*

Gymnasts are used to pushing through discomfort.

You train tired.

You compete sore.

You trust yourself to recover.

That mindset creates success in sport.

Financially, it can create blind spots.

Debt feels manageable early.

Minimum payments feel small.

Balances feel temporary.

Until they are not.

Debt does not care how disciplined you are in other areas. It only cares whether payments arrive on time and balances decrease.

## *Credit Mistakes That Cost Points*

Most credit damage comes from predictable mistakes.

Late payments.

High credit card balances.

Opening too many accounts too quickly.

Ignoring statements.

Co-signing without understanding the risk.

Using credit to cover lifestyle gaps.

In gymnastics terms, these are execution errors. Not dramatic falls. Small form breaks repeated over time.

Co-signing deserves special attention.

When you co-sign, you are fully responsible.

If the other person misses payments, your score takes the hit.

Your trust is on the line.

That is like putting your name on someone else's routine and hoping they hit it.

## *Why Minimum Payments Are a Trap*

Minimum payments are designed to keep you in debt longer.

They protect the lender, not you.

Paying the minimum is like finishing a routine knowing deductions are locked in. You stay on the floor, but you do not win.

Aggressive repayment restores control.

Slow repayment increases pressure.

## *Coach's Perspective: What Would Your Coach Say?*

A coach would be blunt.

"Stick the landing."

"Control the routine."

"Don't give points away."

"Details matter."

"Finish strong."

Credit is about execution.

Debt is about discipline.

No coach accepts sloppy basics. Financial discipline deserves the same respect.

## *Game Situations and Decision Points*

You can put it on a card.

Does it fit the plan, or is it convenience?

You qualify for a loan.

Do you ask whether you should take it, or just whether you can?

Someone asks you to co-sign.

Do you understand the risk, or feel pressured?

These are deduction moments. Awareness determines the score.

## *Common Athlete Mistakes and Financial Parallels*

Gymnasts rush difficulty.

Financially, that means borrowing before stability.

Gymnasts ignore form.

Financially, that means ignoring balances.

Gymnasts assume talent will save them.

Financially, that means assuming income will fix mistakes.

Talent does not erase deductions.

Neither does income.

## *Winning the Long Game*

Clean routines win meets.

Clean credit histories win flexibility.

Credit is not about avoiding borrowing forever. It is about borrowing with control. Using debt intentionally. Eliminating deductions before they accumulate.

When credit is managed well, it becomes invisible.

When it is mismanaged, it dominates decisions.

The goal is not perfection.

The goal is clean execution.

## *Athlete Takeaways*

- Credit is a scoring system, not a judgment.
- Interest is a deduction that compounds over time.
- Borrow to build, not to impress.
- Small credit mistakes add up quickly.
- Clean execution protects long-term flexibility.

# Chapter 5: The Equipment Check: Banking Basics

Before every meet, there is an equipment check.

Bars are adjusted.

The beam is tested.

The floor is inspected.

Grips are checked.

Tape is tightened.

No one skips this step.

You do not walk onto the competition floor assuming everything will work itself out. A loose grip, a slick beam, or uneven bars can turn a clean routine into a fall. Equipment issues are not dramatic, but they are unforgiving. When something goes wrong, it is never the moment you want to discover it.

Banking is the equipment of your financial life.

It is not exciting.

It does not win medals.

But if it is sloppy, nothing else works the way it should.

Before you think about investing, growth, or long-term goals, your banking system has to function cleanly. If it does not, money leaks quietly through fees, mistakes, stress, and preventable errors.

That is why this chapter matters.

## *Checking vs Savings Accounts*

Checking accounts are for movement.

Savings accounts are for storage.

They are not interchangeable.

Checking is where money flows in and out.

Paychecks.

Bills.

Daily spending.

Automatic payments.

Savings is where money sits with intention.

Emergency funds.

Short-term goals.

Protection.

Future plans.

In gymnastics terms, checking is the competition floor.

Savings is the mat under the apparatus.

You need both.

If everything stays in checking, money is constantly exposed. It gets spent accidentally. It disappears without intention. If everything stays in savings, nothing is happening. You are safe, but not progressing.

Problems arise when people blur the two.

Using one account for everything feels simple, but it creates confusion. You stop knowing what money is available to spend versus what money is meant to protect you. That confusion leads to overdrafts, missed opportunities, and stress.

Separation creates clarity.

Clarity creates control.

### *Why Structure Matters More Than the Bank Name*

Many athletes obsess over where they bank.

Big bank.

Local bank.

Credit union.

Online bank.

The brand matters far less than the structure.

The question is not "Where do I bank?"

The question is "Does my system work?"

A clean system means:

Money moves when it should.

Bills are paid on time.

Savings is protected from spending.

Fees are minimized.

Mistakes are caught quickly.

In gymnastics terms, this is apparatus setup. Different gyms use different equipment brands, but the best gyms all have clean setups. Bars are even. Mats are secure. Systems are intentional.

Your banking setup should feel boring and predictable. That is a good thing.

### *Online Banks vs Traditional Banks*

Traditional banks offer:

Physical branches.

In-person service.

Tellers.

Face-to-face problem solving.

Online banks often offer:

Lower fees.

Higher savings interest rates.

Strong automation.

Convenience.

Neither option is universally better.

The right choice depends on how you operate.

Some athletes like walking into a branch.

Others value efficiency and automation.

Some use a hybrid approach.

In gymnastics terms, this is personal preference in equipment. Some athletes prefer softer beams. Others like firmer floors. What matters is familiarity and reliability.

Where athletes get into trouble is not understanding trade-offs.

Fees.

Transfer timing.

Customer service access.

ATM availability.

Deposit holds.

If you do not know how your bank works, you are trusting equipment you have never tested.

### *How Money Moves Electronically*

Money does not teleport.

It moves through systems.

Direct deposit.

Electronic transfers.

Debit card transactions.

Automatic bill pay.

Peer-to-peer apps.

Each system has timing rules.

Deposits clear at certain times.

Transfers take days, not seconds.

Bills pull money whether you are ready or not.

Most overdrafts happen because people misunderstand timing, not because they are reckless.

In gymnastics terms, this is rhythm and timing. Miss the beat and everything feels rushed. Get the timing right and the routine flows.

Know:

When your paycheck posts.

When bills pull.

How long transfers take.

What time cutoffs apply.

This awareness prevents unnecessary deductions.

### *Why Overdrafts Are Preventable Errors*

Overdrafts feel accidental.

They are not.

They are system failures.

Overdrafts happen when:

Spending exceeds awareness.

Timing is misunderstood.

No buffer exists.

Alerts are ignored.

Banks charge fees for overdrafts because they can. Those fees are penalties for poor execution.

In gymnastics terms, overdrafts are stepping out of bounds. You know the boundary exists. Crossing it costs you.

A simple buffer in checking prevents most overdrafts. Keeping savings separate but accessible provides backup without confusion.

You do not need perfection.

You need margin.

### *Protecting Yourself From Fraud*

Fraud happens when systems are loose.

Cards get skimmed.

Accounts get hacked.

Charges slip through unnoticed.

Most fraud damage occurs not because of the initial charge, but because it goes unnoticed too long.

Protection comes from:

Regular account review.

Transaction alerts.

Strong passwords.

Separate accounts.

Quick response.

In gymnastics terms, this is awareness on the apparatus. If something feels off, you adjust immediately. You do not finish the routine pretending nothing happened.

The faster you act, the less damage occurs.

Fraud is not a moral failure.

It is an operational issue.

Clean systems reduce exposure.

## *Why Alerts Are Not Optional*

Alerts feel annoying.

They are protective.

Low balance alerts.

Large transaction alerts.

Unusual activity alerts.

These are your spotters.

You hope they never need to step in.

When they do, you are glad they are there.

Ignoring alerts is like ignoring a coach yelling corrections mid-routine.

Information exists to help you adjust.

## *Common Banking Mistakes Athletes Make*

Using one account for everything.

Ignoring statements.

Not knowing fees.

Trusting autopay without checking.

Assuming the bank will catch errors.

Leaving no buffer.

In gymnastics terms, these are fundamentals skipped because they feel boring.

Boring fundamentals prevent falls.

## *Coach's Perspective: What Would Your Coach Say?*

A coach would not make this complicated.

"Check your equipment."

"Protect the basics."

"Don't create your own problems."

"Details matter."

"Handle your business."

Banking is not about intelligence.

It is about execution.

Sloppy systems create stress.

Clean systems create freedom.

## *Game Situations and Decision Points*

You get hit with a fee.

Do you adjust the system or shrug it off?

You notice a charge you do not recognize.

Do you act immediately or wait?

You have money in savings but still overdraft checking.

Do you restructure or keep guessing?

These moments decide whether the routine stays clean.

### *Common Athlete Mistakes and Financial Parallels*

Gymnasts ignore equipment.

Financially, that shows up as banking errors.

Gymnasts assume stability.

Financially, that shows up as surprise fees.

Gymnasts skip basics.

Financially, that shows up as chaos.

The same mindset produces the same results.

### *Winning the Long Game*

Clean equipment allows clean routines.

Good banking does not feel exciting.

It feels invisible.

That is success.

When your banking system works:

Money moves when it should.

Savings stays protected.

Mistakes get caught early.

Stress stays low.

That creates space to focus on growth instead of recovery.

### *Athlete Takeaways*

- Checking is for movement. Savings is for protection.
- Separate systems create clarity and control.
- Know how and when your money moves.
- Alerts and buffers prevent costly mistakes.
- Clean banking systems support every financial routine.

# Part II: Stability and Protection

**Strong routines require control and safety.**

In gymnastics, difficulty means nothing without control. You can have the hardest skills in the gym, but if the basics are shaky, falls happen. Spotting, mats, proper equipment, and smart progressions exist for one reason: protection. They allow athletes to train, compete, and improve without one mistake ending everything.

Money works the same way.

This part of the book focuses on protecting what you are building. Not chasing upside. Not adding difficulty. Creating stability so one unexpected event does not knock you off the apparatus. Risk awareness, insurance, and protection strategies are the financial equivalents of safety mats, spotters, and smart training plans.

These chapters are about staying upright when pressure shows up.

When protection is in place, confidence increases. Decisions get clearer. You stop reacting and start executing. Stability is not conservative. It is what allows long careers, clean routines, and strong finishes.

Before you add difficulty, you protect the base.

# Chapter 6: Risk Awareness and Smart Decision Making

Every gymnast remembers the first time a skill felt truly risky.

Not the first time you tried it into a pit or with a spot. The first time you were asked to perform it on the actual apparatus. The mat felt thinner. The margin for error felt smaller. The room felt quieter. Suddenly, your awareness sharpened.

Great gymnasts do not avoid risk. They understand it.

They know when to add difficulty and when to stay clean. They know when a skill fits their readiness and when it threatens the routine. That judgment is what separates reckless attempts from championship routines.

Money requires the same awareness.

Most financial mistakes are not caused by bad math. They are caused by misunderstanding risk. Athletes are comfortable with pressure, which can be an advantage. But without understanding how financial risk actually works, that confidence can quietly turn into exposure.

This chapter is about learning to evaluate risk the way a disciplined gymnast evaluates difficulty.

## *Emotional Risk vs Financial Risk*

Emotional risk is how risk feels.

Financial risk is what risk can do to your life.

Athletes often confuse the two.

You are trained to perform under pressure. You have competed in front of judges, crowds, and teammates. You know how to fall, get back up, and try again. Emotionally, risk feels manageable.

Financially, the consequences are different.

If one bad outcome forces you into debt, eliminates savings, disrupts your career, or causes you to abandon a long-term plan, that risk was too high for your current situation.

In gymnastics terms, this is the difference between *wanting* to compete a skill and being *ready* to compete it.

You may feel confident attempting a release move, but if your grip strength, timing, or consistency are not there yet, the risk outweighs the reward. Confidence does not override readiness.

Financial confidence works the same way.

Feeling comfortable taking risk does not mean your financial life can absorb it. The question is not "Can I handle this emotionally?" The real question is "What happens if this does not go my way?"

### *Time Horizon and Flexibility*

Time horizon is how long your money has to work.

Flexibility is your ability to adjust if something goes wrong.

Together, they determine how much risk you can responsibly take.

If money is needed soon, risk tolerance should be lower. There is no time to recover from a fall. If money is for decades from now, short-term volatility matters less because recovery time exists.

In gymnastics terms, this is competition timing.

You do not debut a new skill the week of championships. Early in the season, you experiment. You fall safely. You adjust. As the meet approaches, you simplify, polish, and protect scores.

Money follows the same pattern.

Early stages allow more experimentation. Later stages require more control.

Flexibility is the hidden variable most people ignore.

Do you have savings?

Stable income?

Low debt?

Support systems?

A gymnast with strong basics and good spotting can push difficulty safely. A gymnast dealing with injury or inconsistency cannot. Financially, flexibility determines how forgiving risk will be.

Ignoring time horizon and flexibility is like performing every routine as if it is the same meet. Context matters.

## *How Risk Affects Every Money Decision*

Risk is not limited to investing.

It affects every part of your financial routine.

How much cash you keep.

How much debt you take on.

What insurance coverage you carry.

How aggressive your lifestyle choices are.

How quickly you commit to long-term obligations.

Risk shows up everywhere.

For example, keeping no emergency savings increases risk even if your investments are conservative. Taking on high fixed expenses reduces flexibility even if income is strong. Skipping insurance exposes you to catastrophic outcomes even if everything else looks stable.

In gymnastics terms, this is ignoring safety basics while focusing only on difficulty.

A routine can look strong until one unexpected moment reveals what was not protected.

Every financial decision should be filtered through one simple question:

What happens if this does not go as planned?

That question does not make you fearful. It makes you prepared.

## *Knowing When to Push Difficulty and When to Stay Clean*

Great gymnasts understand routine composition.

Sometimes the winning strategy is pushing difficulty. Other times, it is executing clean skills with precision. Judges reward balance. They punish unnecessary risk.

Money requires the same judgment.

There are moments when taking more risk makes sense. Investing aggressively early. Starting a business. Changing careers. There are also moments when staying clean matters more. Preserving capital. Reducing debt. Protecting income.

The mistake is operating at one speed all the time.

Some people push difficulty constantly. They chase upside, excitement, and aggressive moves regardless of context. Others stay too conservative for too long, avoiding growth even when conditions support it.

Both approaches break routines.

Financial success comes from situational awareness. Knowing when the routine calls for controlled execution and when it allows progression.

Risk is not something you eliminate. It is something you manage intentionally.

## *Coach's Perspective*

A coach would not debate risk emotionally.

They would say it plainly:

Control what you can control.

Do not rush skills you have not earned.

Protect the routine.

Stay composed.

Finish strong.

Coaches do not reward recklessness. They reward discipline. They understand that one fall can erase an entire meet. Financially, the same truth applies.

Risk is part of the sport. Poor awareness is optional.

## *Game Situations and Decision Points*

You are offered an aggressive investment opportunity.

Do you ask if it fits your timeline, or just if it has upside?

You consider a big financial commitment.

Do you evaluate flexibility if income changes?

You feel confident and want to take more risk.

Do you assess downside, or rely on confidence alone?

These moments mirror competition decisions.

Do you push difficulty today, or stay clean and protect the score?

## *Common Athlete Mistakes and Financial Parallels*

Gymnasts trust confidence over readiness.

Financially, that leads to overexposure.

Gymnasts ignore recovery and flexibility.

Financially, that leads to fragile systems.

Gymnasts chase difficulty to impress.

Financially, that leads to unnecessary risk.

The same habits that cause falls in competition cause stress and setbacks with money.

## *Winning the Long Game*

Risk is unavoidable. Failure is not inevitable.

The gymnasts who succeed long-term respect their limits. They progress intentionally. They protect their bodies and routines. They do not confuse bravery with recklessness.

Financial success works the same way.

You take risks when they fit your stage, your flexibility, and your long-term goals. You stay clean when stability matters more than upside. That balance allows you to keep competing, season after season.

That is not playing scared.

That is playing smart.

## *Athlete Takeaways*

- Confidence does not equal readiness. Know the difference.
- Time horizon determines how much risk you can afford.
- Flexibility protects you when things do not go as planned.
- Push difficulty only when the routine supports it.
- Smart risk keeps you on the apparatus and in the meet.

# Chapter 7: Insurance Fundamentals Every Gymnast Needs

Every gymnast understands this truth early.

You can train perfectly, warm up correctly, and execute with confidence, and still get hurt.

A slip on the beam. A short landing on vault. An over-rotation on floor. Injuries are not a sign of failure. They are part of the sport. That is why gyms invest in mats, spotting, athletic trainers, and medical staff. No one assumes injuries will not happen. They prepare for them.

Insurance plays the same role in your financial life.

You do not buy insurance because you expect something bad to happen. You buy it because you understand that risk exists, even when you do everything right. Insurance is not about fear. It is about protection, stability, and staying in the routine when something unexpected happens.

Gymnasts who ignore safety measures do not look brave. They look careless. Financially, skipping insurance is the same mistake.

## *Health Insurance Basics*

Health insurance is not optional.

It covers doctor visits, prescriptions, emergency care, surgeries, and long-term treatment. Without it, one injury or illness can erase years of financial progress in a matter of weeks.

Athletes often fall into a dangerous mindset here. You are young. You are healthy. You train hard. You feel durable. That mindset works until it does not.

In gymnastics terms, skipping health insurance is like training difficult skills without mats because you "feel good today." You might be fine for a while. When something goes wrong, the consequences are severe.

Health insurance has three core components you must understand:

Premiums are what you pay to keep coverage active.

Deductibles are what you pay out of pocket before insurance starts helping.

Out-of-pocket maximums cap how much you pay in a worst-case year.

The goal is not to eliminate cost. The goal is to cap damage. Health insurance protects you from financial catastrophe so an injury does not become a long-term setback.

Know what plan you have.

Know what it covers.

Know what it does not.

Ignoring the details does not make them disappear.

### *Auto and Renters Insurance*

Auto and renters insurance are two of the most commonly overlooked protections, especially for young athletes and former athletes.

Auto insurance protects you, your vehicle, and everyone else involved in an accident. It covers damage, medical costs, and liability if someone is hurt.

Renters insurance protects your personal property and provides liability coverage if something happens where you live. Fire, theft, water damage, or accidents involving guests can all create major expenses without warning.

In gymnastics terms, these policies protect your balance between skills.

You might be focused on training, school, work, or competition, but one accident outside the gym can disrupt everything. Insurance keeps a mistake or bad luck from turning into a financial fall.

Many athletes view these policies as unnecessary expenses because nothing has gone wrong yet. That logic is flawed.

Accidents do not announce themselves. Protection must exist before it is needed.

### *Homeowners Insurance*

If you own a home, homeowners insurance becomes foundational.

It protects:

The structure itself

Your belongings

Your liability exposure

It also covers events people rarely consider until they happen. Fires. Storm damage. Accidents. Lawsuits. Major repairs.

Owning property without insurance is like performing a full routine without mats during warmups. Everything feels fine until one unexpected moment exposes what was not protected.

Homeowners insurance is not about making money. It is about preventing a total loss from wiping out your progress. It is defense. Quiet, boring, essential defense.

### *Deductibles, Premiums, and Coverage Limits*

This is where confusion usually starts.

Premiums are what you pay consistently.

Deductibles are what you pay before insurance helps.

Coverage limits are the maximum the policy will pay.

Higher deductibles usually mean lower premiums. Lower deductibles usually mean higher premiums. There is no perfect option. There is only balance.

In gymnastics terms, this is routine construction.

You do not load every skill with maximum difficulty if consistency suffers. You choose combinations that you can execute reliably under pressure. Insurance works the same way. You want coverage you can afford to maintain and deductibles you can handle without panic.

Insurance is not about getting every dollar back. It is about limiting how bad things can get when something goes wrong.

## *Why Athletes Often Underestimate Insurance*

Athletes are conditioned to trust preparation and effort.

You believe you can control outcomes through discipline. Most of the time, that belief serves you well. Financially, it can create blind spots.

Insurance exists because not everything is controllable.

Illness does not ask permission.

Other drivers make mistakes.

Natural disasters do not care how disciplined you are.

Skipping insurance is not confidence. It is exposure.

Gymnasts respect safety protocols because they understand that risk exists even when execution is clean. Financial maturity means applying that same logic to money.

## *Coach's Perspective*

A coach would not negotiate this.

Protect yourself.

Know the rules.

Do not leave yourself exposed.

Stay available.

Availability matters.

If one unexpected event takes you out financially, the issue was not effort. It was lack of protection. Insurance keeps you in the meet when something goes wrong.

## *Game Situations and Decision Points*

You are healthy and thinking about skipping coverage.

Do you save money today or protect against the unknown?

You choose the cheapest policy available.

Do you understand what it does not cover?

You assume nothing bad will happen.

Are you prepared if it does?

These are risk decisions. Awareness matters more than optimism.

### *Common Athlete Mistakes and Financial Parallels*

Gymnasts underestimate injury risk.

Financially, that means skipping insurance.

Gymnasts focus on difficulty instead of safety.

Financially, that means underinsuring.

Gymnasts ignore details in routines.

Financially, that means surprises when it matters most.

Protection does not feel important until it is missing.

### *Winning the Long Game*

Insurance does not win medals. It keeps careers intact.

It allows you to recover instead of panic. To adjust instead of abandon the routine. To stay composed when something unexpected happens.

You cannot control everything. You can control how prepared you are when it does.

That is balance.

That is discipline.

That is smart gymnastics applied to money.

### *Athlete Takeaways*

- Insurance is financial safety equipment. Use it.
- Health coverage is non-negotiable.
- Auto, renters, and homeowners insurance protect stability.
- Premiums and deductibles are trade-offs. Know yours.
- Staying protected keeps you in the routine when things go wrong.

# Chapter 8: Life, Disability, and Liability Protection

Every gymnast knows this feeling.

You train for years to build strength, flexibility, and control. Your body becomes your engine. Every skill, every routine, every opportunity depends on it working the way it is supposed to. When something goes wrong physically, everything else is affected. Training stops. Competition pauses. Plans change.

Your income works the same way.

Most athletes think about money in terms of what they earn. Very few think about what protects that earning power. Life, disability, and liability insurance exist to protect the foundation underneath everything else. They are not about performance. They are about continuity.

You cannot stick the landing if the routine falls apart halfway through.

## *Why Protection Matters More Than People Think*

Gymnasts are disciplined, resilient, and used to pushing through discomfort. That mindset creates success in sport. Financially, it can create blind spots.

You assume you will always be able to work.

You assume injuries will heal quickly.

You assume nothing major will happen.

Most of the time, those assumptions hold. Insurance exists for the times they do not.

Protection is not pessimism. It is preparation.

## *Term vs Permanent Life Insurance*

Life insurance answers a simple question.

If something happened to you, who would be financially affected?

Life insurance is not about you. It is about the people who depend on your income, your support, or your presence.

**Term life insurance** covers you for a specific period of time. Ten years. Twenty years. Thirty years. It is designed to protect against financial loss during the years when people rely on your income. It is straightforward, affordable, and focused.

**Permanent life insurance** lasts your entire life and includes additional features like cash value. It is more complex and more expensive. For most athletes and young professionals, it is not necessary early on.

In gymnastics terms, term insurance is like using the right skill at the right moment. Clean execution. No extra difficulty. Permanent insurance is a more advanced routine that only makes sense when the foundation is already strong.

The mistake athletes make is assuming life insurance is something to think about later. If someone relies on your income today, protection matters today.

## *Disability Insurance and Income Protection*

This is the most overlooked and most important protection for athletes.

Disability insurance protects your ability to earn income if you cannot work due to injury or illness. It replaces a portion of your income while you recover or adjust.

In gymnastics terms, disability insurance protects the routine when the body cannot perform.

You insure your phone.

You insure your car.

You insure your apartment.

Yet many athletes fail to insure the thing that produces all of those payments. Your income.

Disability is not always permanent. Sometimes it is temporary. A surgery. An illness. A recovery period. Without income protection, those months can create long-term financial damage.

Athletes assume disability is rare. Statistically, it is more common than death during working years. Ignoring it is not confidence. It is exposure.

### *Umbrella Liability Coverage*

Liability is about responsibility.

If someone is injured on your property, harmed in an accident, or sues you for damages, liability coverage protects you. Umbrella insurance provides additional coverage above your auto and homeowners or renters policies.

In gymnastics terms, this is an extra mat underneath the routine.

Most of the time, your primary coverage is enough. When it is not, umbrella coverage prevents a fall from becoming catastrophic.

As athletes progress in careers, build assets, or gain public visibility, liability risk increases. Umbrella coverage is relatively inexpensive for the protection it provides.

It exists for worst-case scenarios, not everyday concerns.

### *How These Policies Work Together*

Life insurance protects others if you are gone.

Disability insurance protects you if you cannot work.

Liability insurance protects what you are building from legal risk.

Together, they form a safety system that supports everything else.

In gymnastics, safety systems do not replace skill. They allow you to train, compete, and progress without unnecessary fear. Financial protection works the same way.

## *Common Insurance Mistakes Athletes Make*

Athletes make predictable mistakes when it comes to protection.

They delay coverage because they feel young and healthy.

They underinsure to save money now.

They buy complex products they do not understand.

They assume employer coverage is enough.

They never review policies as life changes.

In gymnastics terms, this is training advanced skills without checking equipment or understanding the scoring system. It works until it does not.

Insurance mistakes often do not show up immediately. They show up when life changes, when something unexpected happens, or when responsibilities increase.

## *Why Employer Coverage Is Not Enough*

Many athletes rely entirely on employer-provided insurance.

Employer coverage is helpful, but it has limits.

It may not replace enough income.

It may disappear if you change jobs.

It may not cover long-term situations.

Relying solely on employer coverage is like assuming the gym will always spot you. When circumstances change, you need your own protection.

## *Coach's Perspective*

A coach would not debate this.

Protect yourself.

Plan for setbacks.

Do not assume everything goes perfectly.

Stay available.

Coaches prepare athletes for mistakes, injuries, and adversity. Financial protection is preparation for life's version of that adversity.

### *Game Situations and Decision Points*

You have people depending on your income.

Do you protect them or assume nothing will happen?

You rely on your body for work.

Do you protect your income or hope you recover quickly?

You are building assets and visibility.

Do you add protection or ignore liability risk?

These decisions are not emotional. They are situational.

### *Winning the Long Game*

Strong routines are not just about difficulty. They are about control.

Life, disability, and liability insurance do not create wealth. They protect the ability to build it. They keep one unexpected event from undoing years of disciplined work.

Gymnasts understand that preparation happens before competition. Financial protection works the same way.

You do not wait until you fall to add mats.

### *Athlete Takeaways*

- Life insurance protects people who rely on you.
- Disability insurance protects your ability to earn.
- Liability coverage protects what you are building.
- Cheap coverage today can be expensive later.
- Strong routines include safety systems, not just difficulty.

# Part III: Building Difficulty and Value (Investing Fundamentals)

Difficulty is what separates basic routines from competitive ones. But every gymnast learns this early: difficulty only adds value when it is executed well. A harder skill done poorly costs more than it earns. A clean, controlled routine with the right level of difficulty wins more often than reckless upgrades.

Investing works the same way.

Growth does not come from complexity alone. It comes from understanding, control, and repetition. Adding difficulty before mastering fundamentals leads to falls. Adding difficulty with discipline creates long-term progress.

This part of the book focuses on investing fundamentals. Not shortcuts. Not hype. Not flashy tricks. These chapters are about how markets actually work, how risk and return interact, and how to build value gradually without losing balance.

You will learn how ownership works, why volatility is normal, how compounding rewards patience, and why simple, well-executed strategies outperform complicated ones over time. Just like gymnastics, the goal is not to impress in one moment. The goal is to build a routine that holds up season after season.

Difficulty is optional. Control is not.

In the chapters that follow, you will learn how to add the right amount of difficulty to your financial routine, at the right time, in a way that increases your score without risking a fall.

# Chapter 9: How Financial Markets Really Work

Every gymnast remembers the first time a routine fell apart under pressure.

The skills were there. The training was there. But the environment changed. The crowd was louder. The judges were closer. The stakes felt higher. Suddenly, everything felt faster and less predictable.

Financial markets feel the same way from the outside.

To someone watching casually, markets look chaotic. Prices move constantly. Headlines scream urgency. Opinions fly in every direction. It feels unpredictable, emotional, and out of control.

But just like gymnastics, what looks chaotic on the surface is built on structure underneath. There are rules. There are systems. There are patterns. And once you understand them, the noise matters a lot less.

Markets do not exist to confuse you. They exist to function.

## *How Markets Function*

At their core, financial markets are places where ownership and loans are exchanged.

Companies need money to grow. Governments need money to operate. Investors provide that money in exchange for either ownership or interest. Prices move based on expectations about the future, not just what is happening today.

In gymnastics terms, the market is the competition floor. Many athletes perform. Some routines score higher. Some struggle. Judges adjust. Conditions change. But the competition continues meet after meet.

Markets are not designed to feel comfortable. They are designed to allocate capital efficiently. Ups and downs are not malfunctions. They are part of the system.

When you understand that, you stop reacting emotionally to every movement.

## *Stocks, Bonds, and Ownership*

Stocks represent ownership.

When you buy a stock, you are buying a piece of a real business. That business sells products or services, hires employees, competes with others, and tries to grow profits over time. As an owner, you participate in that success or struggle.

Bonds are loans.

When you buy a bond, you are lending money to a government or company. In return, they pay you interest and promise to return your principal later.

In gymnastics terms, stocks are difficulty. They add potential value, but they require control. Bonds are stability. They do not push the score as high, but they help you stay upright when conditions change.

You do not win with difficulty alone. You win by combining difficulty with execution and balance.

Ownership is the key concept. Investing is not betting on price movements. It is owning productive assets over time.

## *Market Cycles and Volatility*

Markets move in cycles.

Growth periods.

Slowdowns.

Declines.

Recoveries.

Then the cycle repeats.

Volatility is movement. Not failure. Price swings feel uncomfortable, but they are normal. Long periods without volatility would be more concerning than reassuring.

In gymnastics terms, this is rhythm and flow. No routine is perfectly still. There are moments of acceleration and moments of control. Losing balance slightly does not mean the routine is over. Panicking does.

Athletes who struggle financially often confuse discomfort with danger. They see volatility and assume something is broken. In reality, volatility is the cost of participating in growth.

The mistake is not experiencing market swings. The mistake is abandoning the routine because of them.

## *Long-Term Strategy vs Risky Shortcuts*

Every gymnast has seen someone chase difficulty too early.

They add skills before their basics are clean. They rush upgrades because others are doing them. Sometimes it works. Often it leads to falls, injuries, or stalled progress.

Financial shortcuts work the same way.

Chasing hot stocks.

Timing the market.

Jumping into trends without understanding.

Trying to outsmart systems designed to punish impatience.

These approaches feel exciting. They also increase risk without increasing control.

Long-term investing is about sustained execution. Consistent contributions. Broad ownership. Discipline through cycles. It is the equivalent of building clean routines year after year instead of gambling on one perfect meet.

Winning financially is not about being right quickly. It is about staying in position long enough for ownership and time to work.

## *Coach's Perspective*

If a coach were talking about markets, the message would sound familiar.

Trust your training.

Do not rush upgrades.

Control what you can control.

Stay composed when things wobble.

Finish the routine.

Markets reward patience, discipline, and repetition. They punish emotion, shortcuts, and ego.

No coach wants an athlete panicking mid-routine. No investor should panic mid-cycle.

## *Game Situations and Decision Points*

The market drops suddenly.

Do you assume failure, or recognize volatility?

You hear about a hot investment.

Do you chase it, or evaluate whether it fits your routine?

You feel behind compared to others.

Do you force difficulty, or stay clean and consistent?

These are the same decisions athletes face in competition. Awareness determines outcomes.

## *Common Athlete Mistakes and Financial Parallels*

Athletes react to crowd noise.

Financially, that leads to emotional investing.

Athletes rush upgrades.

Financially, that leads to risky shortcuts.

Athletes abandon fundamentals under pressure.

Financially, that leads to panic selling.

The habits that create falls in gymnastics create losses in investing.

## *Winning the Long Game*

Markets reward ownership, patience, and discipline. You do not need to predict every move. You need to stay in the routine.

Just like gymnastics careers, financial success is built over seasons, not single meets. Some athletes will experience sudden opportunities or income spikes. The same principles still apply. Without structure, those opportunities disappear quickly.

Difficulty adds value only when executed well.

## *Athlete Takeaways*

- Markets are structured systems, not chaos
- Stocks add growth, bonds add balance
- Volatility is normal, panic is optional
- Ownership beats speculation
- Stay disciplined and finish the routine

# Chapter 10: Risk, Return, and the Power of Compounding

Every gymnast remembers the first time a coach talked about difficulty versus execution.

You could add a harder skill and raise your start value, but only if you could land it consistently. Push too far, too fast, and deductions wiped out any advantage. Play it too safe, and your score stayed capped no matter how clean the routine looked.

Risk and return work the same way with money.

There is no reward without risk, but unmanaged risk does not create progress. It creates falls. Understanding how risk, volatility, and compounding work together is what allows you to build difficulty over time without blowing up the routine.

## *Risk and Reward Tradeoffs*

Every financial decision carries tradeoffs.

Higher potential returns usually come with higher risk.

Lower risk usually means lower expected returns.

That relationship is not a flaw in the system. It *is* the system.

In gymnastics terms, risk and reward are start value and execution. A harder routine gives you more upside, but only if you can stay in control. A simpler routine limits your ceiling but increases consistency.

Financially, this shows up everywhere:

- Stocks have higher long-term growth potential but move around more.
- Bonds provide stability but grow more slowly.
- Cash feels safe but loses purchasing power over time.

The mistake athletes make is thinking one option is "right" and the others are "wrong." Just like gymnastics, the correct mix depends on the athlete, the season, and the goal.

Early in your career, you may be able to handle more difficulty.

Closer to major goals, you may need more control.

Risk is not about bravado. It is about alignment.

## *Volatility vs Permanent Loss*

This is one of the most misunderstood concepts in investing.

Volatility is movement.

Permanent loss is damage.

Markets going up and down is volatility. Losing money because you panic, overextend, or abandon discipline is permanent loss.

In gymnastics terms, volatility is a wobble. Permanent loss is a fall.

Every gymnast wobbles. That does not end the routine. What ends the routine is reacting emotionally to the wobble instead of staying composed.

Athletes often see market drops and assume something is broken. In reality, volatility is the price of admission for growth. It only becomes dangerous when behavior turns short-term movement into long-term mistakes.

Selling at the bottom.

Abandoning a plan after one bad cycle.

Taking on too much risk without protection.

Those are the financial equivalents of stepping off the mat.

## *Compounding Over Time*

Compounding is where everything changes.

Compounding means your money earns returns, and then those returns earn returns. Over time, growth accelerates not because you are doing anything new, but because time is stacking on itself.

In gymnastics terms, compounding is repetition.

One practice does not change much.

One season of consistent training does.

Multiple years of clean reps transform difficulty, confidence, and results.

The same is true financially.

Saving and investing regularly may feel small at first. Progress looks slow. Results seem unimpressive. Then, after enough time, momentum builds and growth becomes visible.

Compounding rewards patience more than brilliance. You do not need perfect timing. You need consistency and time.

## *Why Athletes Are Uniquely Positioned to Benefit*

Athletes already understand compounding intuitively.

You know:

- Progress comes from showing up.
- Small habits matter more than occasional intensity.
- Skipping basics delays everything else.

Financially, that mindset is a massive advantage if you apply it.

Regular contributions.

Staying invested through cycles.

Avoiding emotional decisions.

Letting time do the heavy lifting.

That is compounding in action.

The athletes who struggle are not the ones who lack intelligence. They are the ones who expect immediate results or abandon the plan when growth feels slow.

### *The Real Cost of Waiting*

Waiting feels safe. It feels responsible. It feels patient.

It is not.

Every year you delay investing is a year compounding cannot work for you. Lost time cannot be recovered later by trying to "catch up." Starting earlier with less money almost always beats starting later with more.

In gymnastics terms, skipping foundational years does not get fixed by cramming later. Missed reps are missed reps.

Many athletes wait because:

- They feel behind.
- They want to learn more first.
- They are waiting for the "right time."

There is no perfect time. There is only time already passing.

You do not need to start big. You need to start now.

### *Managing Risk Without Freezing*

Risk does not mean recklessness, and managing risk does not mean avoiding action.

Smart risk management looks like:

- Diversifying instead of betting on one outcome.
- Matching risk to time horizon.
- Keeping emergency funds so investments are not forced to be liquidated.
- Increasing difficulty gradually as confidence and capacity grow.

In gymnastics, you do not add the hardest skill first. You build progressions.

Financially, you do the same.

Risk is something you manage, not something you eliminate.

### *Coach's Perspective*

A coach would be direct.

Reps matter.

Trust the process.

Do not rush upgrades.

Stay composed when things wobble.

Finish strong.

No coach expects perfection every routine. They expect discipline, effort, and consistency. Investing rewards the same behavior.

### *Game Situations and Decision Points*

The market drops.

Do you stop investing, or keep showing up?

You feel behind financially.

Do you force risk, or stay disciplined?

You want to wait for certainty.

Do you start anyway?

The decision you make in these moments determines whether volatility stays temporary or becomes permanent damage.

### *Common Athlete Mistakes and Financial Parallels*

Athletes chase quick progress.

Financially, that leads to over-risking.

Athletes panic after mistakes.

Financially, that leads to selling at the wrong time.

Athletes delay training.

Financially, that leads to lost compounding.

The same behaviors that limit athletic ceilings limit financial ones.

## *Winning the Long Game*

Compounding does not reward perfection. It rewards persistence.

You do not need to win today. You need to stay in the routine long enough for time to work. Some athletes will experience sudden income or opportunities. Without discipline, those moments disappear quickly. With structure, they accelerate everything.

Risk and return are always connected. The goal is not to avoid risk, but to manage it in a way that allows compounding to work uninterrupted.

Finish the routine.

## *Athlete Takeaways*

- Risk and reward are always linked
- Volatility is normal; permanent loss comes from bad decisions
- Compounding rewards consistency, not intensity
- Waiting costs more than starting imperfectly
- Stay disciplined and let time do the work

# Chapter 11: Stocks Without the Flashy Tricks

Every gymnast has seen this happen in a meet.

An athlete adds a flashy skill they are not fully ready for. The crowd reacts. The routine looks impressive for a moment. Then the landing comes, and the deductions erase everything. What could have been a strong, clean score turns into frustration because difficulty replaced execution.

Stocks get treated the same way.

People chase what looks exciting. The hot company. The headline name. The viral story. The promise of quick gains. And just like gymnastics, the flash usually hides weak fundamentals. Winning with stocks is not about tricks. It is about clean execution over time.

## *What Owning Stock Actually Means*

When you buy a stock, you are not buying a symbol on a screen. You are buying ownership in a real business.

That business:

- Sells products or services
- Hires employees
- Makes decisions
- Competes with other companies

- Succeeds or struggles over time

As a shareholder, you own a small piece of that operation. Your results depend on how the business performs over years, not days.

In gymnastics terms, owning stock is committing to a routine, not a single skill. You are judged on the whole performance. One impressive moment does not define success.

This is where many athletes misunderstand stocks. They think in terms of short-term price movement instead of long-term ownership. But investing is not reacting to scores mid-routine. It is trusting the preparation and letting the judges evaluate the full performance.

Stocks reward patience because businesses grow through cycles, not overnight.

## *Growth vs Value Investing*

Growth and value investing are often framed as opposites. In reality, they are different expressions of difficulty and execution.

Growth investing focuses on companies expected to grow faster than average. These companies often reinvest profits to expand, innovate, and capture market share. They attract attention, excitement, and higher expectations.

Value investing focuses on companies that appear undervalued relative to their fundamentals. They may not be exciting. They may not dominate headlines. But they tend to generate steady results.

In gymnastics terms:

- Growth investing is higher difficulty. More upside, more risk, more deductions if execution slips.
- Value investing is cleaner execution. Lower flash, more control, consistent scores.

Championship routines balance difficulty and execution. Portfolios do the same.

Relying only on growth can increase volatility and emotional stress. Relying only on value can limit upside. The goal is not choosing sides. The goal is balance that fits your skill level, time horizon, and tolerance for wobble.

## *Dividends and Total Return*

Dividends are cash payments some companies make to shareholders. They provide income while you hold the stock.

But dividends are not the whole story.

Total return includes:

- Price growth
- Dividends received

Focusing on only one misses the real result.

In gymnastics terms, total return is the full score, not just the difficulty or just the execution. You need both to understand performance.

Some athletes fixate on dividends because they feel tangible. Others ignore them entirely and focus only on price movement. Both miss the point. What matters is how all components work together over time.

A stock that grows steadily without dividends can be just as powerful as one that pays income. A stock that pays dividends but never grows may not keep up with long-term goals.

Total return is the scoreboard that matters.

## *Why Stocks Feel Like Gambling to Athletes*

Many athletes believe stocks are gambling. That belief comes from how stocks are discussed, not how they actually work.

Gambling is guessing outcomes without control, protection, or a plan.

Investing is owning assets with discipline, diversification, and time.

In gymnastics terms, gambling is throwing a skill you have not trained and hoping it works. Investing is building a routine you have practiced thousands of times.

Stocks only feel like gambling when people:

- Chase hot tips
- Trade constantly
- React emotionally to short-term movement
- Ignore fundamentals

When stocks are used correctly, they are boring. Boring is good. Boring is repeatable.

## *Common Investing Myths Athletes Hear*

Athletes hear a lot of bad advice around stocks, especially when income starts to show up.

**Myth: You have to trade constantly to win**

Reality: Frequent trading increases mistakes, taxes, and stress. Ownership over time wins.

**Myth: If the price drops, you failed**

Reality: Volatility is normal. Discipline determines long-term outcomes.

**Myth: You need inside information**

Reality: Markets price information quickly. Fundamentals matter more than secrets.

**Myth: Stocks are only for rich people**

Reality: Stocks reward consistency, not starting size.

**Myth: You can outsmart the market with instincts**

Reality: Emotion is the fastest way to lose control.

These myths persist because they sound confident and exciting. Coaches do not build champions on excitement. They build them on fundamentals.

### *Execution Beats Excitement*

Gymnastics punishes freelancing. So does investing.

Trying to be clever usually leads to mistakes. Trying to be disciplined leads to progress. Stocks reward people who:

- Stay invested
- Diversify
- Avoid emotional decisions
- Let time work

Execution matters more than ideas.

You do not need the perfect stock.

You do not need the perfect timing.

You need a system you can stick with.

### *Coach's Perspective*

A coach would not overcomplicate this.

Stick to what you trained.

Do not chase flash.

Make the routine clean.

Trust the process.

Finish the routine.

Stocks reward fundamentals the same way gymnastics does. When pressure increases, discipline matters more, not less.

### *Game Situations and Decision Points*

A stock you own drops in price.

Do you panic, or remember why you bought it?

You hear about a hot stock.

Do you chase it, or evaluate how it fits your plan?

You feel bored with steady progress.
Do you add unnecessary difficulty, or stay composed?
The moment tests discipline, not intelligence.

### *Common Athlete Mistakes and Financial Parallels*

Athletes chase high difficulty too early.
Financially, that shows up as speculative investing.
Athletes abandon routines after one mistake.
Financially, that shows up as panic selling.
Athletes overestimate instinct and underestimate preparation.
Financially, that leads to ignoring fundamentals.
The same behaviors that cause falls cause financial setbacks.

### *Winning the Long Game*

Stocks are not lottery tickets. They are tools for long-term growth.

When used with discipline, they quietly build wealth over time. When used emotionally, they create stress and regret. The difference is not intelligence. It is execution.

Clean routines win meets.
Clean execution wins financially.

### *Athlete Takeaways*

- Owning stock means owning a real business
- Growth and value both matter when balanced correctly
- Dividends and price growth together tell the real score
- Flashy tricks increase risk without improving results
- Stay disciplined and trust your training

# Chapter 12: Bonds and Maintaining Balance

Every gymnast understands balance is not optional.

You can have strength. You can have flexibility. You can have difficulty. But if you lose balance, the routine unravels quickly. A wobble on the beam costs confidence. A step on the landing costs points. Too many corrections, and the score never recovers.

Balance is not flashy.

It is not exciting.

It is what allows everything else to work.

Bonds play that exact role in investing.

They do not flip.

They do not fly.

They exist to stabilize the routine so the rest of the performance can succeed.

## *How Bonds Work*

A bond is a loan.

When you buy a bond, you are lending money to a government or a company. In return, they agree to:

- Pay you interest over time
- Return your original money at a set maturity date

That is it.

There is no ownership. There is no upside explosion. There is predictability.

In gymnastics terms, bonds are the base you push off of. They are the controlled element that allows harder skills to exist without collapsing the routine.

Stocks aim for growth.

Bonds aim for stability.

Both matter.

Many athletes misunderstand bonds because they compare them to stocks and find them boring. But boredom is not a flaw. Boredom is often the point.

## *Why Bonds Feel Unnecessary When You Are Young*

Early in a career, athletes feel invincible.

Your body recovers fast.

Your time horizon feels endless.

Mistakes feel fixable.

Financially, that mindset often leads athletes to believe bonds are useless. Why choose something steady when you could chase growth?

In gymnastics terms, this is focusing only on difficulty and ignoring execution. It can work for a while. Eventually, deductions catch up.

Bonds are not about maximizing excitement. They are about managing risk so one bad moment does not erase years of work.

## *Interest Rate and Credit Risk*

Bonds come with two primary risks.

**Interest rate risk**

When interest rates rise, existing bond prices usually fall. When rates fall, bond prices usually rise.

In gymnastics terms, this is timing risk. The skill itself is solid, but conditions matter. Even clean execution can look different depending on context.

**Credit risk**

This is the risk that the borrower does not pay you back.

Higher-quality borrowers, like governments or strong companies, usually pay lower interest because they are more reliable. Lower-quality borrowers pay higher interest because there is more risk.

In gymnastics terms, this is trusting the surface you are competing on. A solid mat gives confidence. A shaky surface increases risk, no matter how skilled you are.

Understanding these risks does not mean avoiding bonds. It means choosing the right ones for the role they play.

## *What Bonds Are Not*

Bonds are not designed to:

- Make you rich quickly
- Beat stocks over long periods
- Feel exciting

And that is okay.

Gymnastics routines are not judged on how entertaining they look alone. They are judged on control, consistency, and execution. Bonds support those qualities financially.

Using bonds incorrectly is expecting them to do a job they were never meant to do.

## *When Bonds Make Sense*

Bonds become more valuable as stability becomes more important.

They tend to make sense when:

- You are closer to using the money
- You need predictable income
- You want to reduce volatility
- You want psychological stability during market swings

In gymnastics terms, bonds are about sticking the landing. As the routine progresses, control matters more than adding difficulty.

You do not eliminate hard skills. You support them.

Many athletes wish they had respected balance earlier, not because they regret growth, but because they regret stress they did not need.

## *Bonds as a Shock Absorber*

Markets move.

Stocks swing.

Headlines change.

Emotions spike.

Bonds help absorb that movement.

They often move differently than stocks, which can soften the overall impact of market volatility. That does not mean bonds never fluctuate. It means they often reduce the magnitude of swings.

In gymnastics terms, this is proper landing mechanics. You do not eliminate force. You absorb it so the routine finishes clean.

Without bonds, portfolios can feel like routines with uncontrolled landings. They may score high sometimes. They also risk hard falls.

## *Stability in a Diversified Portfolio*

Diversification is about balance, not complexity.

A well-built portfolio typically includes:

- Stocks for growth
- Bonds for stability

- Cash for flexibility

In gymnastics terms, this is a complete routine. Strength, flexibility, control, and execution working together.

Remove one element, and the routine becomes fragile.

Athletes often overvalue offense and undervalue defense financially. Bonds provide defense. Defense keeps you in position to win.

## *Emotional Benefits of Bonds*

One of the most overlooked benefits of bonds is emotional control.

When portfolios are too aggressive, athletes:

- Panic during downturns
- Second-guess decisions
- Abandon plans at the wrong time

Bonds reduce the emotional swings that lead to bad decisions.

In gymnastics terms, this is confidence built through repetition. When you trust your base, pressure feels manageable.

Bonds help you stay in the routine when others bail.

## *Coach's Perspective*

A coach would not frame this emotionally.

Stay balanced.

Control the routine.

Do not rush.

Protect the landing.

Finish strong.

Bonds are not exciting because they are not meant to be. They exist so you do not beat yourself.

### *Game Situations and Decision Points*

Markets get volatile.

Do you want protection or pure difficulty?

You are approaching a major life goal.

Do you adjust for stability or keep pushing risk?

You feel bored with steady progress.

Do you abandon balance or trust the routine?

These decisions determine outcomes more than market performance.

### *Common Athlete Mistakes and Financial Parallels*

Athletes chase difficulty at the expense of execution.

Financially, that means ignoring bonds.

Athletes underestimate the importance of clean landings.

Financially, that means poor timing.

Athletes confuse boredom with failure.

Financially, that leads to unnecessary risk.

### *Winning the Long Game*

Bonds do not win meets by themselves.

They prevent falls.

They allow growth to compound without interruption. They support discipline when emotions rise. They keep the routine intact when pressure hits.

Championship routines are not reckless.

They are controlled.

## *Athlete Takeaways*

- Bonds are loans designed for stability, not excitement
- Interest rate and credit risk determine how bonds behave
- Bonds matter more as goals get closer
- Stability supports growth, not the other way around
- Clean balance helps you stick the financial landing

# Chapter 13: Funds, ETFs, and Team-Based Investing

Every gymnast knows you do not win meets alone.

Even in individual events, success is built on a team. Coaches. Teammates. Trainers. Judges. Spotters. Training partners. Strength staff. Everyone plays a role. No matter how talented you are, trying to carry everything yourself leads to burnout, mistakes, and inconsistency.

Investing works the same way.

Funds and ETFs are team-based investing. Instead of relying on one company, one stock, or one idea to carry your future, you spread responsibility across many parts working together. That is how you reduce mistakes, control risk, and stay consistent over time.

This chapter is about why team-based investing works, how to use it correctly, and why simplicity usually beats complexity.

## *Why Athletes Are Tempted to Go Solo*

Athletes are trained to believe effort and talent solve problems.

You are used to owning outcomes. If something is not working, you train harder. You fix technique. You take responsibility. That mindset builds champions in sport.

Financially, that same instinct can backfire.

Many athletes believe:

- Picking the right stock is how you win
- If you research enough, you can outsmart the market
- Owning fewer investments means more control

In gymnastics terms, this is trying to perform an entire routine on one skill. It looks impressive in theory. In reality, it is fragile. One mistake ruins everything.

Funds and ETFs remove the need to be perfect.

## *What Funds and ETFs Actually Are*

Mutual funds and ETFs both pool money from many investors and invest it across a collection of stocks or bonds.

Instead of owning one company, you own dozens, hundreds, or even thousands at once.

That is diversification.

In gymnastics terms, this is spreading difficulty across the routine instead of stacking everything into one element. You lower the chance that one mistake destroys the score.

Funds exist to reduce reliance on any single outcome.

## *Mutual Funds vs ETFs*

Both mutual funds and ETFs accomplish the same core goal: diversification. The difference is how they operate.

**Mutual funds**

- Usually trade once per day
- Often actively managed
- Common inside retirement accounts
- May have higher minimum investments

**ETFs**

- Trade throughout the day like stocks
- Often passively managed
- Usually more tax-efficient
- Often lower cost and more flexible

In gymnastics terms, mutual funds are structured training sessions. ETFs are competition-speed reps. Both can work. What matters is understanding how they fit into your system.

There is no universal winner. The right choice depends on where the account is held, how often you trade, and how much complexity you want.

## *Index Investing vs Active Investing*

This is one of the most misunderstood topics in investing.

**Index investing** aims to match market performance. It does not try to beat the market. It focuses on low cost, discipline, and consistency.

**Active investing** tries to outperform the market through manager decisions, timing, and selection.

In gymnastics terms:

- Index investing is clean execution of fundamentals
- Active investing is adding difficulty and risk for higher potential scores

Both exist. Both can work. The difference is reliability.

Most athletes are better served by clean routines executed consistently than by risky difficulty added too early. Index strategies reward patience and discipline. Active strategies require exceptional skill and consistency to justify their cost.

Trying to outsmart the market without experience is like upgrading difficulty before mastering form.

### *Why Index Investing Fits Athletes Well*

Index investing removes ego from the equation.

You do not need to predict which company wins.

You do not need to time the market perfectly.

You do not need constant decisions.

You simply stay invested and let the system work.

In gymnastics terms, this is trusting your training instead of improvising mid-routine. It feels boring. It scores well.

Most long-term investing success comes from staying in position, not from being clever.

### *Fees and Expense Ratios*

Fees matter more than almost anything else.

An expense ratio is the annual cost of running a fund. It might look small, but over time it compounds just like returns.

High fees quietly drain performance.

In gymnastics terms, fees are execution deductions. One small deduction does not seem catastrophic. Repeated deductions destroy the score.

A fund that charges higher fees must outperform just to keep up. Many do not.

Lower fees give you a head start every single year.

### *Why Athletes Often Ignore Fees*

Athletes are conditioned to focus on performance, not cost.

If something looks impressive or exclusive, it feels worth it. Financial products often exploit that mindset. Fancy strategies, complex language, and prestige labels distract from the basics.

In gymnastics, judges do not care how complex the explanation is. They care about execution.

Fees are execution.

## *Diversification Without Complexity*

Diversification does not mean owning everything.

It means owning enough to reduce risk.

You do not need dozens of funds. You need coverage across:

- Different companies
- Different industries
- Different regions
- Different asset types

In gymnastics terms, this is role clarity. Everyone has an assignment. No one tries to cover everything.

Over-diversifying creates confusion. Under-diversifying creates risk. The goal is balance.

Simple systems are easier to maintain under pressure.

## *Why Team-Based Investing Reduces Stress*

One of the biggest benefits of funds and ETFs is emotional control.

When one company struggles, others may perform.

When one sector falls, others may rise.

When headlines get loud, the system keeps working.

In gymnastics terms, this is trusting the routine when nerves spike. You are not improvising. You are executing.

Team-based investing helps athletes avoid the emotional mistakes that derail long-term success.

## *Coach's Perspective*

A coach would not overcomplicate this.

Trust the system.

Do your job.

Stop trying to be the hero.

Execute the fundamentals.

Finish the routine clean.

Funds exist to help you win without needing perfect decisions.

## *Game Situations and Decision Points*

You want excitement.

Do you chase individual stocks or trust a team-based system?

You hear about a high-fee strategy.

Do you understand the cost or just the story?

You feel behind.

Do you add complexity or double down on discipline?

The same choices show up repeatedly. Discipline decides outcomes.

## *Common Athlete Mistakes and Financial Parallels*

Athletes try to do everything themselves.

Financially, that means overtrading.

Athletes chase difficulty before mastering form.

Financially, that means active strategies too early.

Athletes underestimate small mistakes.

Financially, that means ignoring fees.

## *Winning the Long Game*

Team-based investing works because it removes pressure to be perfect.

You do not need to win every day.

You do not need to predict outcomes.

You need to stay consistent.

Funds and ETFs let you focus on behavior instead of predictions. Over time, that discipline compounds.

Championship routines are not reckless.

They are controlled, repeatable, and trusted.

## *Athlete Takeaways*

- Funds and ETFs spread responsibility across a team
- Index strategies reward discipline and consistency
- Fees are silent deductions that compound over time
- Diversification reduces stress and mistakes
- Simple systems hold up best under pressure

# Chapter 14: Real Estate and Alternative Routines

Every gymnast knows that not every skill belongs in every routine. There are specialty elements. High-risk releases. Complex combinations. Skills that can raise the score when performed at the right time, by the right athlete, with the right preparation. But no coach builds a routine around specialty skills before the basics are mastered. If form, balance, and fundamentals are not solid, adding difficulty does not add value. It adds deductions.

Real estate and alternative investments work the same way.

They can strengthen a financial routine. They can add value, diversification, and opportunity. But when they are added too early, too aggressively, or without understanding, they create instability instead of progress.

These are not foundation skills.

They are situational routines.

## *Why Athletes Are Drawn to Real Estate and Alternatives*

Athletes are trained to look for edges.

You are wired to search for advantage. Extra reps. Better equipment. Faster recovery. New training methods. That mindset is powerful. It also makes athletes vulnerable to financial shortcuts that sound like secrets.

Real estate and alternatives are often sold as:

- "How real wealth is built"
- "What successful people do"
- "A way to get out of the stock market"
- "Passive income without effort"

Those statements are not always wrong.

They are often incomplete.

In gymnastics terms, this is being told a difficult skill will boost your score without being shown the deductions if it goes wrong. The upside is highlighted. The risk is minimized.

The problem is not real estate or alternatives themselves.

The problem is timing and fit.

## *Renting vs Owning*

This decision carries more emotion than logic for many athletes.

Owning a home is often framed as a milestone. Renting is framed as temporary or inferior. That framing is wrong.

Renting provides flexibility.

Owning provides stability and long-term potential.

Neither is a trophy. Neither is a failure.

In gymnastics terms, renting is like competing on different apparatuses or training facilities. You can move. Adjust. Adapt. Owning is like committing to a specific routine, surface, and setup long-term.

The right choice depends on:

- Income stability
- Career flexibility
- Location
- Time horizon
- Willingness to manage responsibility

Buying before you are ready is like locking in a routine before you can execute it consistently. The commitment magnifies mistakes.

## *The Hidden Costs of Ownership*

Many athletes focus on the upside of owning and underestimate the responsibility.

Ownership includes:

- Maintenance and repairs
- Property taxes
- Insurance
- Unexpected expenses
- Reduced flexibility
- Time and mental energy

In gymnastics terms, this is adding difficulty without increasing recovery capacity. You might handle it at first. Over time, fatigue shows up.

Ownership can be a powerful move when it fits your routine.

It becomes a burden when it does not.

The mistake is not buying a home.

The mistake is buying one because it feels like the "next step" instead of the right step.

## *REITs and Indirect Ownership*

Real Estate Investment Trusts, or REITs, allow you to invest in real estate without owning property directly.

You get exposure to:

- Commercial buildings
- Apartments
- Offices
- Storage facilities

- Infrastructure

You do not manage tenants.

You do not fix toilets.

You do not negotiate leases.

In gymnastics terms, REITs are being part of the team without running the entire routine yourself. You benefit from performance without carrying the operational load.

REITs can:

- Provide income
- Add diversification
- Preserve liquidity
- Reduce management stress

They still carry risk. Prices move. Income can fluctuate. They are not guaranteed.

REITs often make more sense earlier than direct property ownership because they allow participation without sacrificing flexibility.

## *Why Indirect Ownership Is Often Overlooked*

Athletes often want control.

You are used to hands-on effort producing results. Indirect ownership feels passive. It feels less impressive. It does not come with stories about tenants or renovations.

But control is not always an advantage.

In gymnastics, trusting your coach and system often produces better results than trying to self-correct mid-routine. REITs allow you to stay invested without overextending yourself.

Indirect does not mean inferior.

It often means disciplined.

## *Alternatives Like Commodities and Private Investments*

Alternatives include:

- Commodities
- Private equity
- Private credit
- Hedge strategies
- Other non-traditional assets

They can add diversification. They can also add complexity, risk, and stress.

Alternatives are often:

- Illiquid
- Difficult to value
- Expensive
- Hard to exit
- Complex to understand

In gymnastics terms, these are high-difficulty skills. When executed perfectly, they can change outcomes. When rushed or misunderstood, they create major deductions.

Most athletes do not need alternatives early.

## *Why Alternatives Are Often Used Too Soon*

Alternatives appeal to ego.

They feel sophisticated. They sound exclusive. They promise access and advantage. That attraction leads people to use them before they are ready.

In gymnastics terms, this is adding release moves before mastering basics. The routine looks advanced until it falls apart.

Alternatives should complement a strong foundation.

They should never replace it.

## *Liquidity and Risk Considerations*

Liquidity is how quickly you can access your money without penalty or delay.

Stocks and bonds are generally liquid.

Real estate and alternatives often are not.

When money is illiquid:

- Selling may take time
- Prices may be unfavorable
- Options become limited
- Stress increases

In gymnastics terms, this is being locked into a routine with no room for adjustment. If something changes mid-performance, you cannot adapt.

Before committing to illiquid investments, ask:

- When might I need this money?
- What happens if income changes?
- What if life forces an adjustment?
- How flexible do I need to be?

Ignoring liquidity is one of the fastest ways athletes lose control.

## *Why Liquidity Equals Balance*

Balance is not just physical. It is situational.

Liquidity creates balance because it gives you options. Options reduce stress. Stress leads to mistakes.

Illiquid investments can be powerful when planned correctly. They can also trap you when life changes unexpectedly.

Strong routines allow adjustment without collapse.

Strong financial plans do too.

## *Coach's Perspective*

A coach would be direct.

Master the basics first.

Know the situation.

Do not force difficulty.

Protect balance.

Finish the routine clean.

Specialty skills belong in the right moment, not because they look impressive.

## *Game Situations and Decision Points*

You want to buy property.

Do you understand the full commitment, or just the upside?

You hear about a private deal.

Do you understand liquidity and risk, or just potential returns?

You feel bored with steady progress.

Do you add complexity, or stay disciplined?

Timing matters more than excitement.

## *Common Athlete Mistakes and Financial Parallels*

Athletes rush difficulty.

Financially, that means premature real estate or alternatives.

Athletes underestimate recovery.

Financially, that means liquidity problems.

Athletes chase impressive routines.

Financially, that means unnecessary complexity.

Championship routines avoid forced skills.

## *Winning the Long Game*

Real estate and alternatives are not shortcuts.

They are tools.

When used intentionally, they can strengthen a plan. When used emotionally, they create imbalance.

The goal is not to collect assets.

The goal is to build a routine that holds up under pressure.

Master the basics.

Stick the landings.

Then layer difficulty when it fits.

## *Athlete Takeaways*

- Renting and owning serve different purposes
- REITs provide real estate exposure without operations
- Alternatives add complexity and risk
- Liquidity creates balance and flexibility
- Master fundamentals before adding specialty routines

# Part IV: Managing the Routine (Execution and Adjustments)

Great routines are not rigid. They are controlled.

In gymnastics, even the most carefully constructed routine must adapt in real time. Balance checks happen. Slight adjustments are made mid-skill. Athletes respond to the feel of the apparatus, their own fatigue, and the moment without abandoning form. The goal is not perfection. The goal is clean execution under changing conditions.

Money works the same way.

Once the foundation is built and difficulty is added, success depends on execution and adjustment. Markets move. Life changes. Income shifts. Priorities evolve. The athletes who struggle financially are not the ones who make mistakes. They are the ones who panic, overcorrect, or freeze when conditions change.

Managing your financial routine is about staying composed.

Reviewing without obsessing.

Adjusting without overreacting.

Trusting preparation while responding intelligently to new information.

This part of the book focuses on how to manage what you have built.

How to allocate assets intentionally.

How to buy, hold, and stay disciplined.

How to rebalance without chasing noise.

How to handle pressure, fear, and expectations without losing form.

Just like in gymnastics, the difference between a strong routine and a messy one is not difficulty.

It is execution.

Great routines adjust.

They stay balanced.

And they stick the landing even when conditions are not perfect.

# Chapter 15: Asset Allocation and Routine Composition

Every gymnast knows this truth long before judges ever see a score.

A routine is not just a collection of skills. It is a composition.

You can have world-class difficulty, but if the routine is unbalanced, rushed, or poorly constructed, execution suffers. Too much difficulty early leads to fatigue late. Too little control creates wobbles. Ignoring transitions makes even great skills look sloppy. The best routines are built intentionally, with each element supporting the next.

Asset allocation works the same way.

It is not about picking the single best investment. It is about how all the pieces work together. Stocks, bonds, and cash each play a role. Domestic and international exposure adds depth. Diversification spreads responsibility. And just like gymnastics routines evolve over an athlete's career, asset allocation changes as your life changes.

This chapter is about building a financial routine that holds its form under pressure.

## *Opening Story From Gymnastics*

Think back to learning how to build a full routine.

At first, you focused on individual skills. One tumbling pass. One release move. One dismount. But eventually, the conversation changed. Coaches stopped asking only "Can you do the skill?" and started asking "Where does it belong?"

Too much difficulty back-to-back caused fatigue.

Too much rest killed momentum.

Wrong skill order created unnecessary risk.

A routine is judged as a whole.

Financially, asset allocation is that routine composition. You are not judged on one investment. You live with the outcome of the entire system working together.

## *Stocks, Bonds, and Cash Balance*

Stocks, bonds, and cash are the core elements of your routine.

**Stocks** are growth. They add difficulty and long-term scoring potential. They move. They fluctuate. They are essential for building wealth over time, but they come with risk.

**Bonds** are control and balance. They reduce volatility, provide stability, and help smooth transitions when markets get shaky. They do not steal the spotlight, but they keep the routine upright.

**Cash** is flexibility. It allows you to pause, adjust, and respond to life without forcing moves. Cash is not designed to score points. It exists to protect execution.

In gymnastics terms:

- Stocks are difficulty
- Bonds are control
- Cash is spacing and recovery

A routine overloaded with difficulty may look impressive, but it is fragile. A routine with no difficulty cannot score well. Balance is what allows performance to hold up across an entire season, not just one meet.

## *Why Balance Matters More Than Optimization*

Many athletes approach money the way they approached early competition.

They want the hardest routine.

The biggest upside.

The highest possible score.

That mindset creates financial routines that look impressive on paper but fall apart under stress.

Markets drop.

Life changes.

Income fluctuates.

Emotions show up.

Asset allocation is not about maximizing returns in perfect conditions. It is about surviving imperfect ones without losing form.

In gymnastics, a routine that hits consistently often beats one that swings for perfection and falls half the time. Financial success works the same way.

## *Domestic vs International Exposure*

Most athletes train in familiar gyms, under familiar conditions. But competition does not always happen there.

Different venues.

Different equipment.

Different environments.

Financial markets are global.

**Domestic investments** tie you to your home economy. Familiar companies. Familiar systems. Familiar risks.

**International investments** spread exposure across different countries, economies, and markets. When one region struggles, another may perform differently.

In gymnastics terms, this is competition exposure. Athletes who only train in one environment struggle when conditions change. Those with broader experience adapt faster.

International exposure reduces reliance on any single outcome. It does not eliminate risk. It spreads it.

## *Diversification Principles*

Diversification is often misunderstood.

It does not mean owning everything.

It does not mean eliminating risk.

It does not guarantee better performance every year.

Diversification means spreading responsibility.

In gymnastics, you do not rely on one skill to carry the entire routine. You distribute difficulty, transitions, and execution across the full performance. If one element is slightly off, the routine still holds together.

Financially, diversification spreads exposure across:

- Different companies
- Different industries
- Different asset types
- Different regions

This reduces the chance that one failure ruins everything.

Simple diversification done consistently is far more effective than complex strategies executed emotionally.

## *Career-Stage Allocation*

Gymnastics careers change over time.

Early on, athletes focus on learning skills and building capacity.

Later, routines emphasize control, consistency, and longevity.

Veteran athletes protect their bodies differently than beginners.

Money follows the same arc.

Early in your career, time is your biggest asset. You can afford more volatility because recovery time is long. Growth-focused allocation often makes sense.

As goals get closer, timelines shorten. Stability becomes more important. Bonds and cash often play a larger role. Not because growth is bad, but because mistakes become harder to recover from.

There is no universal "right" allocation.

There is only what fits your stage, your goals, and your life.

Trying to run someone else's routine usually ends poorly.

## *Coach's Perspective*

What would your coach say?

- "Build the routine you can hit, not the one that looks cool on paper."
- "Balance wins meets."
- "Control the basics before pushing difficulty."
- "You don't get bonus points for unnecessary risk."
- "How you train is how you compete."

Asset allocation rewards discipline, not bravado. Clean routines score over time.

## *Game Situations and Decision Points*

- Markets are volatile. Do you panic and change everything, or trust the structure you built?
- You hear someone else's allocation sounds more aggressive. Do you copy it, or stay in your routine?
- Your life changes. Do you adjust allocation intentionally, or ignore reality?

Every decision is a composition choice. One move affects the entire routine.

## *Common Athlete Mistakes and Financial Parallels*

Athletes chase difficulty too early.

Financially, that leads to excessive risk.

Athletes ignore balance.

Financially, that creates stress and instability.

Athletes copy others' routines.

Financially, that leads to misalignment.

The same mistakes that cause falls in competition cause financial setbacks later.

## *Winning the Long Game*

Asset allocation is not exciting.

It is effective.

It allows you to stay invested during downturns.

It reduces emotional decision-making.

It keeps your routine intact when conditions change.

Just like gymnastics, long-term success comes from routines you can execute repeatedly, not routines built for one perfect moment.

## *Athlete Takeaways*

- Build a routine that balances difficulty, control, and recovery
- Stocks, bonds, and cash each have a role
- Diversification spreads responsibility across the routine
- Allocation should evolve as your career evolves
- Clean execution over time beats chasing perfect scores

# Chapter 16: Buying, Holding, and Trusting Your Training

Every gymnast remembers the first time a routine finally felt automatic.

You had trained the skills for years. You had drilled the connections endlessly. You had fallen, corrected, and repeated the same movements until they lived in your body instead of your head. Then one day, in competition, something shifted. You stopped thinking about every step. You trusted the training and executed.

That moment did not happen because you learned something new. It happened because you stopped interfering with what you already knew.

Investing works the same way.

Buying, holding, and trusting your plan sounds simple. In practice, it is one of the hardest parts of money. Not because it is complex, but because emotions show up when the lights are on. Fear. Excitement. Comparison. Doubt. These are the same forces that cause rushed landings and unnecessary adjustments mid-routine.

This chapter is about execution. About doing the work, trusting the reps, and not abandoning your routine when pressure hits.

## *Opening Story From Gymnastics*

Think about competition day.

You warm up. The equipment feels slightly different. The arena is louder. Judges are closer. Your body feels a little tighter than in practice. There is always a moment where instinct whispers, "Adjust something. Play it safe. Change the plan."

Great gymnasts recognize that moment and do not listen to it.

They do not add difficulty.

They do not remove skills.

They do not reinvent the routine.

They trust the training.

Financially, buying and holding is that same decision. You execute what you prepared for, not what your emotions suggest in the moment.

## *Opening and Funding Accounts*

Opening an investment account is easy.

Funding it consistently is the hard part.

Many athletes open accounts the way they buy equipment. They feel productive. They check the box. Then nothing happens. An unfunded account does not grow. It does not compound. It does nothing.

In gymnastics terms, opening an account is joining the gym. Funding it is showing up every day.

Progress only happens with reps.

Consistency matters more than the perfect account type, the perfect timing, or the perfect investment. An average plan executed consistently beats a great plan executed sporadically.

The goal is simple:

- Open the account
- Fund it regularly
- Remove friction so you keep showing up

Automation is your best training partner. Scheduled contributions create discipline when motivation fades.

## *Market Orders vs Limit Orders*

Market orders and limit orders are tools, not strategies.

A **market order** buys or sells immediately at the current price. It prioritizes execution over precision.

A **limit order** sets a specific price and only executes if the market reaches it. It prioritizes control over immediacy.

In gymnastics terms, this is tempo.

Sometimes you move immediately. You trust the moment and commit.

Sometimes you wait for the right setup before initiating.

The mistake is overthinking the tool instead of understanding the purpose.

Many athletes get stuck here. They delay investing because they are waiting for the perfect entry point. They watch prices. They hesitate. They miss reps.

Over time, hesitation costs more than imperfect execution.

## *Buy-and-Hold Discipline*

Buy-and-hold is not about being passive.

It is about being disciplined.

It means you invest with a long-term plan and allow time to do the work. Markets move. Prices fluctuate. That movement is normal.

In gymnastics terms, this is staying on your routine when a skill feels slightly off. You do not stop mid-routine. You do not panic. You keep moving forward and trust your preparation.

Buy-and-hold works because compounding needs time. Interrupting the process breaks momentum.

Most investing underperformance does not come from bad investments. It comes from abandoning the plan at the wrong time.

## *Why Time Matters More Than Timing*

Athletes understand this intuitively.

One missed practice matters far less than months of inconsistent training. Long-term progress comes from staying in the system, not perfect sessions.

Financially, time in the market matters more than timing the market.

Trying to predict short-term movements is like trying to predict judges' scores mid-routine. It adds stress and rarely improves outcomes.

Staying invested allows compounding to work quietly in the background, just like strength gains that show up months later.

## *Avoiding Emotional Decisions*

Emotion is the biggest threat to execution.

Fear during downturns.

Excitement during rallies.

Comparison when others talk about wins.

Pressure to act because "something is happening."

In gymnastics terms, this is crowd noise. The audience reacts. Other athletes hit routines. Judges confer. None of that changes what you need to do next.

Emotional investing leads to:

- Selling low out of fear
- Buying high out of excitement
- Constant changes that disrupt progress

Systems protect discipline when emotions fluctuate. Automation. Rebalancing rules. Long-term plans. These systems remove decision-making from moments of stress.

You do not decide your routine mid-air. You execute what was planned.

## *Trusting the Process When It Feels Uncomfortable*

Every gymnast knows discomfort does not mean danger.

A routine can feel off and still score well. A landing can feel heavy and still stick. Experience teaches you not to overreact to sensation.

Markets feel uncomfortable by design. Volatility is the price of growth. Avoiding discomfort usually leads to worse outcomes than enduring it.

Trust is built before competition. Discipline is tested during it.

## *Coach's Perspective*

What would your coach say?

- "Trust your training."
- "You've done the work."
- "Stick the routine."
- "One skill at a time."
- "Don't beat yourself."

Coaches do not allow athletes to rewrite routines mid-meet. Financial discipline deserves the same respect.

## *Game Situations and Decision Points*

- Markets drop sharply. Do you abandon the plan or stay invested?
- Markets rise quickly. Do you chase excitement or stay disciplined?
- You feel unsure. Do you pause, or do you trust the system you built?

These moments define outcomes. Execution matters more than intelligence.

### *Common Athlete Mistakes and Financial Parallels*

Athletes second-guess routines.

Financially, that leads to poor timing.

Athletes overreact to mistakes.

Financially, that leads to emotional trades.

Athletes abandon structure under pressure.

Financially, that leads to inconsistency.

The same behaviors that cost points in competition cost money later.

### *Winning the Long Game*

Buying and holding is not exciting.

It is effective.

It allows compounding to work.

It reduces emotional errors.

It rewards patience and consistency.

Just like gymnastics, long-term success comes from trusting what you trained for, not chasing perfection in the moment.

### *Athlete Takeaways*

- Open accounts, but more importantly, fund them consistently
- Tools matter less than execution
- Buy-and-hold rewards patience and discipline
- Emotions disrupt routines and portfolios
- Trust your training and finish the routine

# Chapter 17: Rebalancing and Mid-Routine Adjustments

Every gymnast knows this feeling.

You are halfway through a routine. One element was slightly off. Maybe the connection felt rushed. Maybe the landing was heavier than expected. There is a split second where instinct kicks in and tells you to change everything. Slow down. Speed up. Cut a skill. Overcorrect.

Great gymnasts do not do that.

They make small adjustments. They stay composed. They trust the routine. They understand that one imperfect moment does not require a complete reset. Overreacting is how routines unravel.

Rebalancing in investing works the same way.

It is not about fixing mistakes. It is not about reacting to every movement. It is about maintaining balance as conditions change, without losing form, confidence, or discipline.

## *Opening Story From Gymnastics*

Think about training during a long season.

Your body changes. Strength increases. Flexibility fluctuates. Small aches show up. If you never adjust, you break down. If you adjust too much, you lose consistency.

Coaches watch closely.

They do not overhaul routines every week. They make targeted corrections. They shift training emphasis. They protect what is working while correcting what is drifting.

That is rebalancing.

Financially, rebalancing is how you keep your portfolio aligned with your plan as markets move and life evolves.

### *How Often to Review Investments*

There are two common mistakes athletes make with money.

Checking too often.

Not checking at all.

Constant checking creates anxiety. Every fluctuation feels personal. You start reacting emotionally instead of strategically.

Never checking allows drift. Over time, your portfolio can look very different from what you intended, without you realizing it.

The right approach is periodic review.

In gymnastics terms, this is film review.

You do not stop mid-routine to review film. You also do not ignore film for an entire season. You review regularly, calmly, and with purpose.

For most people, reviewing investments once or twice a year is enough. The goal is alignment, not obsession.

### *What Rebalancing Actually Means*

Rebalancing is adjusting your investments back to their intended mix.

Over time, some assets grow faster than others. Stocks may rise faster than bonds. One area of the market may outperform. Without adjustment, your portfolio becomes unbalanced.

Rebalancing trims what has grown beyond its role and adds to what has fallen behind.

In gymnastics terms, this is restoring balance.

If one skill starts dominating the routine at the expense of form, you adjust. You do not eliminate the skill. You put it back in its proper place.

Rebalancing enforces discipline automatically. It removes emotion from decisions and replaces it with structure.

### *Why Rebalancing Feels Uncomfortable*

Rebalancing often feels backward.

It asks you to reduce what has been doing well and support what has struggled. Emotionally, that feels wrong. Logically, it preserves balance.

In gymnastics terms, this is trusting form over flash.

Just because a skill looks impressive does not mean it should take over the routine. Judges reward control, execution, and balance.

Rebalancing is not about predicting the future. It is about respecting the structure you designed.

### *Common Rebalancing Strategies*

There is no single correct method, but the principles are consistent.

Some people rebalance on a schedule, such as annually. Others rebalance when allocations drift beyond certain ranges.

The key is having a rule before emotion enters the picture.

In gymnastics terms, this is predetermined correction.

You decide in practice how you will respond to certain errors. You do not improvise under pressure.

Rules protect discipline.

### *Life Changes and Portfolio Updates*

Rebalancing is not only about markets. It is also about life.

Life changes require adjustments:

- New jobs
- Income changes
- Family responsibilities

- Health changes
- Shifting goals

Ignoring these changes leads to misalignment.

In gymnastics terms, this is forcing an old routine onto a new body. What worked at one stage may not fit later.

As your life evolves, your portfolio should evolve with it. That does not mean constant change. It means intentional updates when circumstances shift.

### *Career Stage and Adjustment*

Early in a career, time absorbs mistakes. Growth often matters more than stability. Later, protection becomes more important.

In gymnastics terms, this is progression.

You do not train the same way at every stage. Beginners focus on basics. Advanced athletes add difficulty. Veterans protect longevity.

Rebalancing helps reflect where you are now, not where you were before.

### *Avoiding Over-Correction*

Over-adjustment is as dangerous as neglect.

Constant tinkering creates instability. Confidence erodes. Discipline disappears.

In gymnastics terms, this is changing the routine every meet. Athletes lose trust in execution and start guessing.

Small, intentional corrections preserve confidence. Big emotional changes usually create problems.

The goal is clean execution, not perfection.

### *Emotional Triggers That Cause Over-Correction*

Certain moments tempt athletes to overreact:

- Sharp market drops
- Rapid market gains
- News headlines
- Other people's success stories

These moments feel urgent. They are rarely actionable.

Rebalancing exists to protect you from reacting to noise. It keeps decisions boring, consistent, and effective.

Boring is good.

### *Coach's Perspective*

What would your coach say?

- "Stay composed."
- "Trust the routine."
- "Make the correction, not the excuse."
- "One skill does not define the routine."
- "Finish strong."

Coaches value athletes who respond calmly, not emotionally.

Financial discipline rewards the same behavior.

### *Game Situations and Decision Points*

- Markets move sharply. Do you rebalance or react emotionally?
- Life changes. Do you update the plan or ignore misalignment?
- You feel uncertain. Do you simplify or complicate?

Each decision mirrors a mid-routine moment. Awareness determines outcome.

### *Common Athlete Mistakes and Financial Parallels*

Athletes overcorrect small mistakes.

Financially, that leads to constant tinkering.

Athletes avoid review.

Financially, that leads to drift.

Athletes panic mid-routine.

Financially, that leads to poor timing.

The same behaviors that cost points in competition cost money later.

### *Why Rebalancing Protects Confidence*

Rebalancing reinforces trust.

It reminds you that you have a plan.

It reduces emotional decision-making.

It keeps risk aligned with reality.

Confidence grows when systems work without constant intervention.

### *Winning the Long Game*

Rebalancing keeps routines clean and portfolios aligned.

It protects progress while allowing growth. It prevents small drifts from becoming big problems. It rewards patience, not prediction.

Long-term success is not about perfect execution. It is about staying balanced through change.

### *Athlete Takeaways*

- Review periodically, not constantly
- Rebalancing restores balance, not perfection
- Life changes require plan updates
- Over-correction creates instability
- Stay composed and trust the routine

# Chapter 18: The Mental Side of Money

Every gymnast knows this moment.

You are standing at the end of the mat. The crowd is loud. Judges are watching. Your heart rate is up. You know the routine. You have trained it thousands of times. But in that moment, your mind gets loud.

What if I miss?

What if I fall?

What if this is not good enough?

The routine has not changed. The pressure has.

Money works the same way.

Most financial mistakes are not caused by a lack of knowledge. They are caused by what happens in your head under pressure. Fear, perfectionism, comparison, and noise quietly influence decisions long before logic gets involved.

The mental side of money is where most routines break down.

## *Opening Story From Gymnastics*

Think about a meet where you were technically ready but mentally tight.

Your form was solid in practice. Your skills were consistent. But once the lights came on, everything felt rushed. You gripped too hard. You hesitated. You overthought.

That was not a physical failure. It was mental interference.

Financially, the same thing happens. People abandon good plans not because the plan is wrong, but because pressure disrupts execution.

## *Fear, Pressure, and Perfectionism*

Fear shows up in different ways.

Fear of losing money.

Fear of making the wrong decision.

Fear of starting too late.

Fear of not being good enough.

Perfectionism often hides underneath fear.

"I need the perfect plan before I start."

"I will invest once I understand everything."

"I do not want to mess this up."

In gymnastics terms, this is waiting for the perfect routine before competing. That moment never comes.

Perfectionism delays action. Fear freezes progress. Together, they keep athletes stuck.

Money does not require perfection. It requires participation.

## *Why Athletes Are Especially Vulnerable*

Athletes are trained to care deeply about outcomes.

Scores matter.

Results matter.

Mistakes are visible.

That mindset builds excellence in sport. It can create paralysis with money.

In gymnastics, one fall feels catastrophic. Financially, small setbacks feel the same way, even when they are normal.

Markets go up and down.

Budgets fluctuate.

Plans evolve.

These are not failures. They are part of the process.

Athletes who expect flawless execution financially often quit when reality shows up.

### *Crowd Noise and Expectations*

In gymnastics, crowd noise is real.

Parents.

Teammates.

Judges.

Social media.

Money has its own crowd noise.

News headlines.

Friends talking about wins.

Influencers.

Family opinions.

Online hype.

Most of this noise has nothing to do with your situation.

In gymnastics terms, reacting to crowd noise instead of listening to your internal cues leads to mistakes. Financially, reacting to noise leads to bad timing, chasing trends, and abandoning plans.

Noise is constant.

Discipline filters it out.

### *Comparison Is the Quiet Destroyer*

Comparison creeps in easily.

Someone else bought a house.

Someone else made money investing.

Someone else seems ahead.

In gymnastics, comparison ruins execution. You rush difficulty. You abandon form. You forget your routine.

Financially, comparison causes people to take risks that do not fit them. They copy strategies without understanding context. They chase outcomes instead of building systems.

Comparison shifts focus from progress to pressure.

Your plan should be built around your routine, not someone else's highlight reel.

## *Building Systems for Discipline*

Discipline fails when it relies on motivation.

Motivation fluctuates.

Emotion changes.

Confidence comes and goes.

Systems protect discipline when motivation fades.

Automation.

Rules.

Checklists.

Scheduled reviews.

Clear boundaries.

In gymnastics terms, this is choreography.

You do not decide what to do mid-routine. You execute what was planned.

Systems remove emotion from decisions.

Saving automatically.

Investing on a schedule.

Rebalancing by rule.

Spending with structure.

These systems keep you moving forward even when you do not feel like it.

## *Why Systems Matter More Than Willpower*

Willpower is unreliable.

You will be tired.

You will be stressed.

You will feel pressure.

Systems do not care how you feel.

In gymnastics, routines do not change based on mood. You rely on training.

Financially, systems are training applied to real life.

The more decisions you automate, the fewer mistakes you make under stress.

### *Staying Composed After Mistakes*

Mistakes will happen.

Overspending.

Missing a contribution.

Making a poor choice.

Losing money temporarily.

What matters is the response.

Overreacting compounds damage.

Ignoring mistakes allows patterns to form.

In gymnastics terms, one wobble does not end a routine unless you panic. You reset and keep moving.

Financial composure means correcting calmly, learning, and continuing forward.

You do not quit the sport after one fall. Do not quit the plan after one mistake.

### *Emotional Triggers That Break Discipline*

Certain moments test mental discipline:

- Market downturns
- Sudden income changes
- Unexpected expenses
- Public success stories
- Financial setbacks

These moments feel urgent. They are rarely emergencies.

Strong performers pause.

Weak performers react.

Pausing creates space for good decisions.

## *Coach's Perspective*

What would your coach say?

- "Control what you can control."
- "Next skill."
- "Stay composed."
- "Do not flinch."
- "Finish the routine."

Coaches do not expect perfection. They expect composure.

Mental discipline is what separates consistent performers from emotional ones.

## *Game Situations and Decision Points*

- You see others doing better. Do you compare or stay focused?
- You make a financial mistake. Do you spiral or reset?
- You feel pressure to act. Do you pause or rush?

Mental choices shape outcomes more than knowledge ever will.

## *Common Athlete Mistakes and Financial Parallels*

Athletes chase perfect routines.

Financially, that leads to inaction.

Athletes react emotionally.

Financially, that leads to poor timing.

Athletes lose confidence after mistakes.

Financially, that leads to quitting.

The same habits that cost points in competition cost progress with money.

### *Why Mental Discipline Creates Freedom*

Mental discipline reduces stress.

Stress creates clarity.

Clarity creates consistency.

When systems are in place and emotions are managed, money stops feeling overwhelming. It becomes another routine you know how to execute.

Confidence grows from repetition, not outcomes.

### *Winning the Long Game*

Money is not won by brilliance. It is won by composure.

When you control emotion, block out noise, trust systems, and stay disciplined, progress continues even through setbacks.

Perfect scores are rare.

Clean routines win over time.

### *Athlete Takeaways*

- Fear and perfectionism delay progress
- Crowd noise distorts decision-making
- Systems protect discipline when motivation fades
- Mistakes require correction, not panic
- Composure keeps the routine intact

# Part V: The Long Career and Sticking the Landing

Every gymnast knows this truth.

Difficulty gets the attention, but landings decide the score.

You can perform a beautiful routine. Clean form. Strong execution. But if you rush the ending, lose focus, or fail to control the landing, everything before it gets discounted. Judges remember how you finish.

Money works the same way.

Early financial decisions matter, but long-term outcomes are determined by how well you manage the later stages of life. Taxes. Career transitions. Big purchases. Retirement. Family responsibilities. These are not flashy skills. They are control skills. They require patience, awareness, and precision.

This part of the book is about longevity.

Gymnastics careers teach you how quickly things change. Bodies change. Roles change. Priorities shift. Financial life follows the same arc. What worked in your early twenties may not work in your forties. What felt optional early becomes essential later.

Sticking the landing financially means:

- Planning beyond the next meet
- Adjusting without losing balance
- Protecting progress you already built
- Making decisions with the end in mind

This is where many athletes struggle.

They trained hard.

They sacrificed.

They did the difficult work early.

Then life sped up.

Careers changed.

Families grew.

Responsibilities multiplied.

Without intention, strong starts turn into messy finishes.

Part V focuses on control, foresight, and execution under long-term pressure. It is about managing money through career transitions, protecting income, handling taxes efficiently, making smart housing and lifestyle decisions, and building independence that lasts long after competition ends.

Just like gymnastics, success here is not about pushing difficulty. It is about precision.

Clean decisions.

Balanced choices.

Strong finishes.

The routines in this section are not designed to impress anyone else. They are designed to support your life when pressure is highest and time matters most.

This is how you turn years of disciplined effort into a confident, controlled landing.

# Chapter 19: Taxes and Where You Hold Your Score

Every gymnast knows this moment.

You finish the routine feeling strong. Difficulty hit. Connections held. Landings controlled. But then the score comes up lower than expected. Not because the routine was bad, but because of small deductions you did not fully account for. A leg separation here. A step there. Nothing dramatic. Enough to matter.

Taxes work the same way.

Most athletes focus on how much they earn, invest, or save. Very few pay attention to where that money lives and how it is scored. Over time, taxes quietly take points off the board. Not through one big mistake, but through small, repeated inefficiencies that compound year after year.

This chapter is about understanding how taxes interact with your money so more of your effort actually counts.

## *Taxable vs Tax-Advantaged Accounts*

Not all accounts are scored the same.

Taxable accounts are flexible. You can add money, take money out, and use it whenever you want. The trade-off is that taxes apply along the way. Interest, dividends, and investment gains may be taxed each year.

Tax-advantaged accounts are structured. They offer tax benefits in exchange for rules. Retirement accounts, health savings accounts, and certain education accounts fall into this category. You may get tax breaks now, later, or both, depending on the account.

In gymnastics terms, taxable accounts are like open training. You have freedom, but mistakes show up immediately. Tax-advantaged accounts are like structured routines. There are rules and restrictions, but when executed correctly, the scoring favors you.

Neither type is bad. They serve different purposes. Problems arise when athletes use the wrong account for the wrong goal.

Short-term money placed into long-term restricted accounts creates frustration. Long-term money left in fully taxable accounts creates unnecessary deductions.

Where you hold the score matters.

## *Tax-Deferred vs Tax-Free Growth*

This is one of the most misunderstood areas of personal finance.

Tax-deferred growth means you delay paying taxes until later. Contributions may reduce taxes today, but withdrawals in the future are taxed as income.

Tax-free growth means you pay taxes upfront, but future growth and qualified withdrawals are not taxed at all.

In gymnastics terms, tax-deferred growth is like pacing difficulty later in the routine. You conserve energy early and pay the cost at the end. Tax-free growth is front-loading effort so the dismount is cleaner and more controlled.

Neither approach is automatically better.

The right choice depends on:

- Current income level
- Expected future income
- Time horizon
- Flexibility needs
- Risk tolerance around future tax rates

Many athletes make the mistake of assuming lower taxes now is always best. Others assume tax-free growth is always superior. Both ignore context.

Smart routines are built around the full sequence, not just the opening skill.

## *Asset Location Basics*

Asset location is not about what you invest in. It is about where you place those investments.

Different assets create different types of tax exposure. Some generate frequent taxable income. Others grow quietly over time. Placing the wrong asset in the wrong account creates unnecessary drag.

In gymnastics terms, this is placement on the apparatus. You do not perform the same skill in the same way on every event. Positioning matters.

For example:

- Investments that generate frequent income may be better placed in tax-advantaged accounts
- Investments focused on long-term growth may benefit from tax-free structures
- Highly flexible money may belong in taxable accounts despite the tax cost

Small decisions here compound quietly. Most people never notice the deductions, but they feel the impact years later.

Asset location is one of the simplest ways to improve results without increasing risk.

## *Common Tax Mistakes Athletes Make*

Most tax mistakes are not aggressive or illegal. They are passive.

They come from avoidance, not intent.

Common issues include:

- Ignoring taxes until filing season
- Using only taxable accounts because they feel easier
- Not understanding how investments generate taxable income
- Assuming future income will always be lower
- Avoiding planning because taxes feel overwhelming

In gymnastics terms, this is losing form because no one is watching closely. Nothing dramatic happens. Scores just quietly suffer.

Taxes do not need to be optimized perfectly. They need to be respected consistently.

Avoiding the topic does not make it go away. It just guarantees more deductions.

## *Why Taxes Matter More Over Time*

Early in your career, taxes may not feel significant. Income may be lower. Assets may be smaller. Mistakes feel manageable.

Over time, the impact grows.

As income increases, tax efficiency matters more.

As assets grow, placement matters more.

As timelines shorten, mistakes become harder to recover from.

In gymnastics terms, early routines allow more margin. Later routines require precision. There is less room to absorb errors.

Understanding taxes is not about obsession. It is about awareness.

You do not need to master the code. You need to understand where deductions come from and how to reduce unnecessary ones.

## *Coach's Perspective*

A coach would frame it simply.

Control what you can control.

Do not give points away.

Understand how you are being scored.

Finish clean.

No coach accepts deductions that come from laziness or lack of awareness. Financially, taxes work the same way.

You cannot avoid scoring. You can choose how prepared you are for it.

## *Game Situations and Decision Points*

You earn more income. Do you adjust where money goes, or keep the same structure out of habit?

You invest for the long term. Do you consider tax impact, or only potential return?

You avoid looking at taxes because they feel complicated. Do you stay uncomfortable now, or pay for it later?

These decisions shape outcomes more than most athletes realize.

## *Common Athlete Mistakes and Financial Parallels*

Athletes focus only on difficulty.

Financially, that means ignoring taxes.

Athletes avoid uncomfortable feedback.

Financially, that means avoiding tax planning.

Athletes rush the ending.

Financially, that means poor withdrawal and account decisions.

Small deductions compound.

## *Winning the Long Game*

Taxes are not the enemy. Ignorance is.

When you understand how accounts are scored, you can place your effort where it counts most. You do not need perfect execution. You need intentional structure.

Strong routines finish clean because they respect the rules.

Financial independence works the same way.

## *Athlete Takeaways*

- Where your money lives affects how it is scored
- Tax-deferred and tax-free growth serve different roles
- Asset placement reduces unnecessary deductions
- Avoidance costs more than imperfection
- Clean finishes come from understanding the scoring system

# Chapter 20: Retirement Accounts and Financial Independence

Every gymnast remembers the first time they trained for a routine that was not about today's meet.

The work felt different. Less adrenaline. More repetition. More patience. You drilled basics that would not pay off immediately. Handstands. Core holds. Landing mechanics. At the time, it felt slow and almost boring. Later, it became obvious why it mattered. When pressure hit, your body already knew what to do.

Retirement planning works the same way.

Financial independence is not built with last-minute effort. It is built through years of quiet preparation, consistent reps, and systems that work even when motivation fades. Retirement accounts are not exciting, but they are foundational. They are where long-term stability is trained long before it is needed.

This chapter is about understanding those accounts, how they work, and how they support a strong financial landing.

## *What Retirement Really Means for Athletes*

Retirement is often misunderstood.

It does not mean stopping work entirely. It does not mean sitting still. It means reaching a point where money is no longer the primary constraint on your choices. You can work because you want to, not because you have to.

In gymnastics terms, financial independence is sticking the dismount under control. You are not rushing. You are not scrambling. You finish on your feet because the routine was built correctly from the start.

Retirement accounts exist to support that outcome. They reward patience, consistency, and structure, not intensity.

## *Employer Plans and Pensions*

For many athletes, the first retirement account they encounter is through an employer.

Employer plans allow you to contribute directly from your paycheck. Money moves automatically before you ever see it. That structure matters.

Some employers also offer matching contributions. That is additional money added on your behalf when you contribute.

In gymnastics terms, this is having access to a well-equipped training facility. You still have to show up and do the work, but the environment makes it easier to progress.

Pensions are less common today, but they still exist in certain careers. They provide income later based on years of service and earnings history. They are structured and predictable, but usually inflexible.

The key lesson is this. If your employer offers a plan, use it intentionally. Ignoring it is like training without equipment that is already available to you.

## *Traditional and Roth IRAs*

Individual Retirement Accounts allow you to save for the future outside of an employer plan.

Traditional IRAs generally provide tax benefits now, with taxes paid later when money is withdrawn.

Roth IRAs work in the opposite direction. You pay taxes upfront, and qualified growth and withdrawals are tax free.

In gymnastics terms, this is choosing how you distribute effort across the routine. Traditional accounts conserve energy early but require more control at the end. Roth accounts demand effort early so the finish is cleaner.

Neither option is universally better. The right choice depends on income level, career stage, and long-term flexibility needs.

Many athletes make the mistake of choosing based on what sounds better instead of what fits their situation. Smart routines are built around context, not trends.

## *Contribution Rules and Discipline*

Retirement accounts come with limits. You can only contribute so much each year. That is not a punishment. It is structure.

Structure creates consistency.

In gymnastics, you do not train every skill every day. You follow a plan that balances volume, recovery, and progression. Retirement contributions work the same way. Small, regular contributions outperform sporadic effort.

Automating contributions removes emotion. You are not deciding every month whether to show up. You already committed.

Discipline here matters more than timing. Trying to maximize contributions perfectly is less important than contributing consistently over long periods.

Reps matter.

## *Withdrawal Rules and Patience*

Retirement accounts are designed for later use. Taking money out early often comes with penalties and taxes.

This is intentional.

In gymnastics terms, this is staying on the apparatus until the routine is complete. Jumping off early may feel relieving, but it destroys the score.

Early withdrawals break compounding. They turn long-term systems into short-term fixes. Many athletes underestimate how costly that interruption can be.

Retirement accounts reward patience. They assume you will let the system work.

That does not mean the money is untouchable. It means it should be treated with respect and clear intent.

## *Retirement Income Basics*

Eventually, retirement accounts shift from accumulation to distribution.

The goal is not a single number. The goal is sustainable income. Money that supports your life year after year without forcing panic or drastic adjustments.

In gymnastics terms, this is landing under control and holding the finish. Not hopping. Not wobbling. Not rushing off the mat.

Retirement income comes from a combination of sources. Accounts, investments, pensions, and personal savings may all play a role.

The earlier you understand this, the more intentionally you can build toward it.

## *Why Athletes Struggle With Retirement Planning*

Athletes are trained for the short term.

You prepare for the next meet. The next season. The next opportunity. That mindset wins competitions. Financially, it can create blind spots.

Retirement feels distant. Abstract. Easy to postpone.

But postponement has a cost. Time is the most valuable training partner you have. You cannot add it back later.

The athletes who succeed financially treat retirement planning like base training. Not glamorous. Not urgent. Essential.

## *Coach's Perspective*

A coach would not overcomplicate this.

Show up.

Do the reps.

Trust the process.

Do not quit early.

Retirement accounts exist because they work. Not because they are exciting.

Discipline beats intensity. Every time.

## *Game Situations and Decision Points*

You get access to an employer plan. Do you enroll immediately or wait?

You hear conflicting advice about Roth versus Traditional. Do you learn the basics or avoid the decision?

You want to use retirement money for a short-term goal. Do you protect the routine or break it?

These decisions shape outcomes long before retirement arrives.

## *Common Athlete Mistakes and Financial Parallels*

Athletes focus only on current meets.

Financially, that means ignoring retirement.

Athletes chase difficulty too early.

Financially, that means skipping foundations.

Athletes quit routines when tired.

Financially, that means stopping contributions.

Long careers are built through patience.

## *Winning the Long Game*

Financial independence is not achieved through brilliance. It is achieved through structure, repetition, and restraint.

Retirement accounts are not about predicting the future. They are about preparing for it.

You do not need to know exactly how life will unfold. You need systems that support you no matter what.

That is how strong landings are built.

## *Athlete Takeaways*

- Retirement is freedom, not inactivity
- Employer plans and IRAs are long-term training tools
- Contribution consistency matters more than perfection
- Early withdrawals break the routine
- Build now so the finish stays clean

# Chapter 21: Housing and Big Financial Decisions

Every gymnast knows the difference between a skill you *can* do and a skill you are *ready* to compete.

You might land it once in practice. Maybe twice. But your coach does not rush to put it in the routine. They watch consistency. They watch recovery. They watch what happens when you are tired, distracted, or under pressure. Big skills are not about capability. They are about readiness.

Housing and major purchases work the same way.

Buying a home. Financing a car. Taking on long-term payments. These decisions are not just about whether you qualify. They are about whether your financial routine is strong enough to support them without wobbling later.

This chapter is about learning when to move forward, when to wait, and how to avoid deductions that show up years after the purchase.

## Renting vs Buying

Renting and buying are often framed as opposites, with one labeled "smart" and the other labeled "wasting money." That framing is wrong.

Renting provides flexibility.

Buying provides stability and long-term potential.

Neither is a trophy. Neither is a failure.

In gymnastics terms, renting is like training without committing a new skill to competition. You can adjust. You can change gyms, coaches, or routines without being locked in. Buying is like committing a skill to your routine. You gain value when it works, but you accept responsibility when it does not.

### *When Renting Makes Sense*

Renting often makes sense when:

- Income is variable or uncertain
- Career location may change
- You want lower responsibility
- You are rebuilding financial basics

Renting keeps your routine lighter. Fewer fixed obligations. Fewer surprises. More room to adjust.

Many former athletes rush to buy because it feels like progress. In reality, buying before you are ready is like adding difficulty without control. It looks impressive until it costs you later.

### *When Buying Makes Sense*

Buying often makes sense when:

- Income is stable
- You plan to stay in one place
- You have emergency savings
- You can handle repairs and maintenance

Buying adds responsibility, but it can also add equity over time.

The key is not the label. The key is fit. A routine should match the gymnast performing it. A housing decision should match the life you are actually living, not the one you feel pressured to show.

## Mortgages and Down Payments

A mortgage is a long-term loan used to purchase a home. It is one of the largest financial commitments most people ever make.

In gymnastics terms, a mortgage is committing to the full routine. Once you step onto the floor, you are in it.

### *Down Payments*

The down payment is your upfront commitment. The more you put down, the less you borrow. That usually means lower monthly payments and less interest over time.

But putting every dollar you have into a down payment can be dangerous.

Liquidity matters.

If buying a home empties your savings, one unexpected expense can turn excitement into stress. A strong routine always leaves margin for error.

### *Monthly Payments Are Not the Full Cost*

Many athletes focus only on the monthly mortgage payment. That is a mistake.

Homeownership also includes:

- Property taxes
- Insurance
- Maintenance and repairs
- Utilities
- Unexpected issues

In gymnastics terms, this is ignoring deductions until they show up on the score sheet. The skill itself is not the whole routine.

Before buying, you need to understand the *total* cost of ownership, not just the payment you qualify for.

## Cars, Leases, and Financing Traps

Cars are one of the fastest ways athletes lose financial balance.

They are emotional purchases. Status-driven. Easy to justify. Heavily marketed.

In gymnastics terms, a car purchase is like choosing music and choreography that looks impressive but drains energy before the dismount.

### *Buying vs Leasing*

Buying a car means ownership. Eventually, the payments stop. You build equity in the sense that you own the asset outright.

Leasing means lower payments and newer vehicles, but no ownership at the end. You are always making payments.

Neither option is automatically wrong. The danger is choosing based on monthly payment alone.

Low monthly payments often hide:

- Longer loan terms
- Higher interest
- Constant replacement cycles

That keeps you stuck in perpetual obligation.

### *Financing Traps*

Common traps include:

- Stretching loan terms to "afford" more car
- Rolling old debt into new loans
- Ignoring total interest paid
- Upgrading vehicles too frequently

These traps quietly limit flexibility.

In gymnastics terms, this is adding difficulty every season without improving basics. Eventually, something breaks.

Cars should support your life, not quietly control it.

## Planning Major Purchases

Big purchases are not isolated events. They interact with everything else in your financial routine.

Before committing, ask:

- Does this reduce or increase flexibility?
- What happens if income changes?
- What am I giving up to afford this?
- Does this align with my long-term goals?

Planning is not pessimism. It is professionalism.

### *The Cost of Rushing*

Many former athletes rush major purchases because:

- They finally have income
- They feel behind compared to peers
- They want proof they "made it"

That urgency creates mistakes.

In gymnastics, rushing difficulty is how falls happen. Financially, rushing purchases creates long-term stress that outlasts the excitement.

## Lifestyle vs Leverage

Housing and cars are not just expenses. They are leverage.

Used correctly, they support your life. Used poorly, they limit it.

A beautiful house that forces stress every month is not a win. A luxury car that delays savings, increases debt, and removes flexibility is not success.

Winning financially often looks boring from the outside. Stable. Controlled. Intentional.

That is what holds up over time.

## Coach's Perspective

A coach would be clear.

Do not rush difficulty.

Make sure the basics are solid.

Protect your landing.

Do not chase scores at the expense of control.

Big decisions require calm evaluation, not emotional momentum.

## Game Situations and Decision Points

You qualify for a bigger loan. Do you take it, or ask what fits your routine?

You want a new car. Do you check total cost, or focus only on the payment?

You feel pressure to "settle down." Do you follow your timeline or someone else's?

Just like gymnastics, discipline shows up in quiet choices long before competition.

## Common Athlete Mistakes and Financial Parallels

Athletes rush upgrades.

Financially, that means overbuying.

Athletes ignore recovery.

Financially, that means no cash buffer.

Athletes chase appearance over execution.

Financially, that means lifestyle traps.

Falls rarely come from one big mistake. They come from ignoring fundamentals.

## Winning the Long Game

Housing and major purchases should support your routine, not dominate it.

The goal is not to own the most. The goal is to live with control, flexibility, and confidence.

Strong gymnasts finish routines they can handle. Strong financial plans do the same.

Stick landings first. Add difficulty later.

## Athlete Takeaways

- Renting and buying are tools, not trophies
- Mortgages and cars create long-term commitments
- Monthly payments hide total cost
- Flexibility matters more than appearance
- Do not rush difficulty before you can stick the landing

# Chapter 22: Your Career Is Your Training Cycle

Every gymnast understands the rhythm of a training cycle.

There is an offseason where you build strength and clean up basics. A preseason where routines take shape. A competition phase where execution matters. And recovery phases where rest, rehab, and adjustment are just as important as work.

Careers work the same way.

The mistake many former athletes make is treating their career like a single meet instead of a long training cycle. They judge success by one job title, one paycheck, or one promotion, instead of understanding how each phase builds toward long-term stability and independence.

Your career is not a single routine. It is a progression of cycles. When you understand that, money decisions around work, benefits, and income make far more sense.

## Salary vs Total Compensation

Most people focus on salary because it is visible.

It is the number on the offer letter. The number people talk about. The number that feels like the score.

But salary is not the full routine.

Total compensation includes everything you receive in exchange for your work:

- Base pay
- Bonuses or commissions
- Health insurance
- Retirement contributions
- Paid time off
- Disability coverage
- Stock options or profit sharing
- Flexibility and work-life structure

In gymnastics terms, salary is one skill. Total compensation is the entire routine score.

Two jobs with the same salary can produce very different outcomes depending on benefits. A slightly lower salary with strong benefits can leave you better protected, healthier, and further ahead long term.

Athletes are trained to look at the scoreboard. Financially, you have to learn to read the judges' sheets too.

### *Why Athletes Miss This*

Former athletes often miss total compensation because:

- Benefits feel abstract
- They were never responsible for insurance before
- Retirement feels far away
- Cash feels more urgent than protection

That is normal. But ignoring benefits is like ignoring form deductions. They do not show up immediately, but they matter over time.

A strong training cycle balances effort, recovery, and protection. A strong career does the same.

## Job Changes and Benefits

Job changes are part of most careers now. Rarely does someone stay with one organization for decades.

The mistake is treating job changes as isolated upgrades instead of system adjustments.

Every job change impacts:

- Income
- Benefits
- Stability
- Stress
- Long-term trajectory

In gymnastics terms, switching jobs is like changing coaches or training environments. It can be positive, but only if you understand what you are gaining and what you are giving up.

### *Benefits Gaps*

One of the most dangerous transitions is a benefits gap.

You leave a job and:

- Health insurance changes
- Retirement contributions pause
- Disability coverage disappears
- Income timing shifts

If you are not prepared, these gaps create pressure. Pressure leads to rushed decisions. Rushed decisions create deductions.

Before changing jobs, ask:

- When does new insurance start?

- Is there a waiting period?
- What happens to retirement accounts?
- How will income timing change?

Elite gymnasts do not change routines without understanding how it affects execution. Careers deserve the same care.

## Negotiation Basics

Negotiation scares many former athletes.

It feels uncomfortable. Personal. Risky.

But athletes negotiate all the time without calling it that.

You negotiate roles.

You negotiate routines.

You negotiate expectations.

You negotiate recovery needs.

Negotiation is not confrontation. It is communication.

### *What You Can Negotiate*

Many people think negotiation only applies to salary. In reality, you can often discuss:

- Salary
- Start date
- Bonus structure
- Paid time off
- Remote or flexible work
- Professional development support

In gymnastics terms, this is adjusting difficulty and composition. You are shaping a routine you can execute well, not just accepting whatever is handed to you.

### *How to Approach Negotiation*

Good negotiation is calm and prepared.

You do not demand.

You do not apologize.

You ask questions.

You explain value.

You listen.

Preparation matters more than bravado.

Know your role.

Know your market.

Know what matters most to you.

Just like competition, confidence comes from preparation, not ego.

## Side Income and Entrepreneurship

Many athletes are drawn to side income.

It feels familiar. Multiple revenue streams. Control. Opportunity.

Side income can be powerful. It can also become a distraction.

In gymnastics terms, side income is adding an extra event. It can raise your all-around score, or it can dilute focus and increase injury risk.

### *When Side Income Makes Sense*

Side income often makes sense when:

- Your primary income is stable
- You have time and energy
- You understand taxes and cash flow
- You are building a skill or asset

Side income should support your training cycle, not exhaust it.

*Common Mistakes*

Athletes often:

- Underestimate time commitment
- Ignore taxes
- Mix personal and business money
- Chase hype instead of skill development

That is like adding difficulty without conditioning. It looks good until execution breaks down.

Entrepreneurship is not a shortcut. It is another long training cycle.

## Career Seasons and Adjustments

Careers have seasons.

Early career is about learning, exposure, and skill development.

Mid-career is about leverage, growth, and optimization.

Later career is about stability, flexibility, and control.

The mistake is expecting every season to feel the same.

Early career income may be lower.

Mid-career stress may be higher.

Later career decisions may prioritize time over money.

That is not failure. That is progression.

In gymnastics, routines evolve as athletes age. Careers should too.

## Coach's Perspective

A coach would frame it clearly.

Train for the long season.

Do not peak too early.

Protect your body and your future.

Make adjustments when needed.

Finish strong.

Careers reward patience, preparation, and smart transitions.

## Game Situations and Decision Points

You get a job offer with higher pay but worse benefits. Do you compare total compensation or just salary?

You feel burned out. Do you change jobs immediately or adjust workload and expectations first?

You want side income. Do you build it intentionally or jump in emotionally?

Every decision is part of the training cycle.

## Common Athlete Mistakes and Financial Parallels

Athletes chase the next competition.

Financially, that means job hopping without strategy.

Athletes ignore recovery.

Financially, that means burnout and stress.

Athletes confuse activity with progress.

Financially, that means side hustles without direction.

Execution matters more than motion.

## Winning the Long Game

Your career funds everything else.

It supports saving.

It supports investing.

It supports freedom later.

Treat it like training, not a scramble.

Strong gymnasts plan cycles.

Strong professionals do the same.

When you align income, benefits, growth, and flexibility, money stops feeling chaotic and starts feeling manageable.

That is how you stay in control long after competition ends.

## Athlete Takeaways

- Salary is one skill, total compensation is the full routine
- Job changes affect more than pay
- Negotiation is preparation, not confrontation
- Side income should support, not exhaust, your system
- Careers are long training cycles, not single meets

# Chapter 23: Estate Planning Basics Everyone Needs

Every gymnast learns this lesson early.

You do not train only for the skill you are doing today. You train so that when something goes wrong, you are protected. You condition to prevent injury. You drill basics so mistakes do not cascade. You plan routines so one wobble does not turn into a fall.

Estate planning works the same way.

Most people think estate planning is about death. That misunderstanding keeps them from doing it. Estate planning is really about control, protection, and continuity while you are alive, and clarity when you are not.

It is not morbid.

It is not complicated by default.

It is not only for wealthy people.

It is foundational planning that prevents chaos when life inevitably throws something unexpected.

## What Estate Planning Actually Is

Estate planning answers four simple questions:

Who makes decisions if I cannot?

Who receives my assets?

How are those assets transferred?

What rules guide those decisions?

Without answers, the system defaults to the courts, the state, and confusion.

In gymnastics terms, estate planning is setting your routine composition in advance. If you do not submit a routine, the judges do not guess what you meant to do. They apply the default rules. Those rules are rarely what you would have chosen.

Estate planning is how you submit your routine before the meet begins.

## Wills and Trusts

### *Wills*

A will is a written set of instructions that explains:

- Who inherits your assets
- Who is responsible for managing your estate
- Who should care for minor children

A will only applies after death. It does not avoid court involvement. It simply gives direction to the probate process.

In gymnastics terms, a will is your routine card. It tells everyone what you intended, even if execution happens later.

Without a will:

- State law decides who receives assets
- Guardianship decisions may not align with your wishes
- Delays and costs increase

A will is not about perfection. It is about clarity.

### *Trusts*

A trust is a legal structure that holds assets and distributes them according to rules you set.

Trusts can:

- Avoid probate
- Provide privacy
- Control timing of distributions
- Protect beneficiaries from poor decisions or outside risks

In gymnastics terms, a trust is like training systems that run even when you are not present. The rules are baked in, and execution continues smoothly.

Trusts are not only for the ultra-wealthy. They are tools. Whether you need one depends on:

- Family complexity
- Asset types
- Privacy concerns
- Control preferences

The key is fit, not status.

## Beneficiaries and Account Titling

This is where most estate plans quietly break.

Beneficiary designations override wills.

Retirement accounts.

Life insurance.

Some bank and investment accounts.

If beneficiaries are outdated, incorrect, or missing, assets may go to the wrong place regardless of what your will says.

In gymnastics terms, this is like executing a clean routine but submitting the wrong start value. The performance does not matter if the paperwork is wrong.

### *Common Athlete Mistakes*

- Never updating beneficiaries after life changes
- Listing parents or ex-partners by default
- Forgetting contingent beneficiaries
- Assuming the will controls everything

Account titling also matters.

Joint accounts.

Individual accounts.

Trust-owned accounts.

Each title carries different rules for access and transfer. These details are boring, but boring details prevent catastrophic deductions.

## Powers of Attorney

Estate planning is not only about death. It is about incapacity.

If you are alive but unable to make decisions due to injury, illness, or accident, someone needs legal authority to act on your behalf.

A power of attorney allows someone you choose to:

- Pay bills
- Manage accounts
- Make financial decisions

Without it, loved ones may need court approval to help you. That process takes time, money, and energy at exactly the wrong moment.

In gymnastics terms, this is assigning a backup when you are injured. You do not wait until you are hurt to decide who fills the role.

### *Financial vs Medical Authority*

Powers of attorney often come in two forms:

- Financial
- Medical

Each serves a different purpose. Both matter.

## Healthcare Directives

Healthcare decisions are deeply personal.

A healthcare directive explains:

- What medical treatments you want or do not want
- Who makes decisions if you cannot
- How end-of-life care should be handled

This is not about pessimism. It is about dignity and clarity.

In gymnastics terms, this is knowing when to stop a routine to prevent serious injury. It is respecting limits and making decisions before emotions take over.

Without directives:

- Loved ones may disagree
- Decisions may be delayed
- Stress compounds

Clear instructions remove guilt and confusion from people you care about.

## Why Athletes Avoid Estate Planning

Athletes often avoid estate planning because:

- They feel young and healthy
- It feels uncomfortable
- It seems unnecessary
- No one around them talks about it

But athletes understand preparation better than most.

You do not skip conditioning because you feel good today.

You do not ignore injury prevention because you feel invincible.

Estate planning is preventative care for your financial life.

## Coach's Perspective

A coach would not hesitate.

Protect yourself.

Handle your business.

Do not leave your team guessing.

Prepare for what you cannot control.

Estate planning is not fear-based.

It is discipline-based.

## Game Situations and Decision Points

You have assets but no will. Do you trust the default rules?

You experience a major life change. Do you update beneficiaries or assume everything carries over?

You become temporarily incapacitated. Does someone have legal authority to help you?

These are not theoretical situations. They happen every day.

## Common Athlete Mistakes and Financial Parallels

Athletes assume nothing will go wrong.

Financially, that leads to no plan.

Athletes avoid uncomfortable conversations.

Financially, that creates confusion later.

Athletes focus on training, not protection.

Financially, that leaves gaps.

Preparation prevents regret.

## Winning the Long Game

Estate planning is not about controlling everything. It is about removing unnecessary chaos.

It ensures:

- Your wishes are followed
- Your people are protected
- Your assets move efficiently
- Your legacy is intentional

Just like gymnastics, the goal is not perfection. The goal is sticking the landing when it matters most.

## Athlete Takeaways

- Estate planning is protection, not pessimism
- Wills and trusts provide clarity and control
- Beneficiaries override intentions if ignored
- Powers of attorney and healthcare directives protect you while alive
- Prepare now so others are not forced to guess later

# Chapter 24: Talking About Money With Family

Every gymnast knows this feeling.

You step onto the floor, but you are not alone. Your coach is watching. Your teammates are watching. Your parents are watching. Sometimes their presence gives you confidence. Sometimes it adds pressure. Either way, relationships change how you perform.

Money works the same way.

Very few financial decisions exist in isolation. Family influences how you think, how you spend, how you save, and how you define success. Yet money is one of the least talked about topics inside families. Silence creates assumptions. Assumptions create tension. Tension leads to mistakes that linger for years.

Talking about money with family is not about control. It is about communication, clarity, and boundaries.

## Why Money Conversations Feel So Hard

Athletes are used to feedback.

You get corrections in real time. You review film. You talk openly about performance. But money conversations feel different because they mix emotion, identity, history, and expectation.

Family money conversations often carry:

- Guilt
- Fear
- Comparison
- Unspoken rules
- Old wounds

In gymnastics terms, it is like performing a routine while thinking about past falls. The hesitation shows up even if the skill is clean.

Avoiding these conversations does not eliminate the pressure. It just forces you to perform without alignment.

## Teaching Kids About Money

Teaching kids about money is not about lectures. It is about exposure and repetition.

Kids learn money the same way they learn movement:

- By watching
- By copying
- By practicing in low-stakes environments

You do not teach a child a full routine on day one. You teach shapes. Basics. Balance. Timing.

Money works the same way.

### *Age-Appropriate Lessons*

For younger kids:

- Money comes from work
- Choices have trade-offs
- Saving means waiting
- Spending is intentional

For older kids:

- Budgeting basics
- Banking and debit cards
- Credit responsibility
- Long-term thinking

In gymnastics terms, this is progressive difficulty. You do not skip levels.

The biggest lesson kids absorb is behavior, not words. How you handle stress, spending, generosity, and planning teaches more than any explanation.

## College Students and Young Adults

This stage is where many athletes feel the gap most sharply.

Structure disappears.

Schedules loosen.

Support systems fade.

Real money decisions show up fast.

College and early adulthood are financial transition phases. Mistakes here do not usually destroy lives, but they shape habits that compound for decades.

### *What Young Adults Need Most*

They need:

- Context, not control
- Guidance, not judgment
- Systems, not lectures

In gymnastics terms, this is the phase where the coach steps back but stays available. Too much control creates rebellion. No guidance creates confusion.

Helpful conversations focus on:

- Cash flow awareness
- Credit basics
- Student loans and obligations
- Lifestyle inflation
- Long-term consequences

The goal is not to eliminate mistakes. The goal is to reduce catastrophic ones.

## Aging Parents and Caregiving

This is the conversation many people avoid the longest and regret the most.

As parents age, roles shift. Financial decisions may need support. Health issues may arise. Responsibilities may change quickly.

Avoiding these conversations does not preserve dignity. It creates chaos when urgency hits.

### *Topics That Matter*

- Healthcare wishes
- Powers of attorney
- Financial access
- Living arrangements
- Long-term care expectations

In gymnastics terms, this is planning for injury prevention and recovery. You do not wait until someone is hurt to discuss protocols.

These conversations are emotional. That does not make them optional.

Clarity now protects relationships later.

## Family Expectations and Boundaries

This is where most financial stress lives.

Expectations around:

- Financial support
- Shared expenses
- Gifts versus obligations
- Helping versus enabling

Boundaries are not rejection. They are structure.

In gymnastics terms, boundaries are the lines on the floor. They allow freedom of movement without chaos.

### *Common Athlete Challenges*

Former athletes often struggle with:

- Feeling pressure to help everyone
- Confusing generosity with responsibility
- Saying yes to avoid conflict
- Carrying guilt about success

Healthy boundaries answer one key question:

What am I responsible for, and what am I not?

Clear boundaries protect both sides of the relationship.

## How to Have Better Money Conversations

You do not need perfect language. You need intention.

Helpful principles:

- Pick calm moments, not crisis moments

- Focus on shared goals
- Use facts, not accusations
- Listen as much as you speak
- Revisit conversations over time

In gymnastics terms, this is like refining a routine over multiple practices. One conversation rarely solves everything.

Progress happens through repetition.

## Coach's Perspective

A coach would be blunt.

Communicate.

Protect the team.

Do not let silence create mistakes.

Handle uncomfortable reps now to avoid falls later.

Money conversations are uncomfortable because they matter.

## Game Situations and Decision Points

Your child asks about money. Do you avoid the topic or invite curiosity?

Your college-age athlete makes a financial mistake. Do you shame or teach?

Your parent resists planning. Do you delay or gently push for clarity?

Just like competition, timing and tone matter.

## Common Athlete Mistakes and Financial Parallels

Athletes avoid tough conversations.

Financially, that leads to assumptions.

Athletes try to carry the team alone.

Financially, that leads to burnout.

Athletes confuse loyalty with silence.

Financially, that leads to resentment.

Communication prevents breakdowns.

## Winning the Long Game

Strong families do not avoid hard conversations. They navigate them with respect and clarity.

Money conversations are not about winning arguments. They are about protecting relationships, reducing stress, and aligning expectations.

Just like gymnastics, success is not about one perfect routine. It is about consistency, trust, and finishing together.

## Athlete Takeaways

- Money conversations are part of team dynamics
- Teach fundamentals early and often
- Guide young adults without controlling them
- Address aging parent issues before crisis hits
- Boundaries create stability, not conflict

# Part VI: Long-Term Success

Long-term success is not about difficulty.

It is about consistency.

In gymnastics, the athletes who last are not always the ones with the highest peak difficulty. They are the ones who stay healthy, manage pressure, adapt as their bodies change, and keep refining fundamentals long after the spotlight fades. Careers end, but habits remain.

Money works the same way.

By this point in the book, you have learned the mechanics. You understand cash flow, risk, investing, protection, taxes, and planning. You know how the system works. What separates people from here forward is not knowledge. It is behavior over time.

Part VI is about staying upright when the routine gets long.

This phase of life looks different for everyone. Some athletes experience early income and visibility. Others grind quietly for years. Some transition smoothly into new careers. Others struggle with identity, direction, or comparison. The financial challenges are not identical, but the principles are.

Long-term success comes from:

- Making decisions that still work when circumstances change
- Avoiding shortcuts that feel good now but cost you later
- Knowing when to ask for help instead of guessing
- Protecting what you have built from avoidable mistakes

This part of the book is about durability.

It is about recognizing that money decisions compound just like training habits. Small errors repeated over time become major deductions. Small disciplines repeated over time create stability, freedom, and options.

You will also learn that the biggest financial threats are not market crashes or bad luck. They are bad advice, unchecked ego, silence, and scams that prey on confidence without education.

Long-term success is not about being perfect. Gymnasts fall. Markets drop. Careers change. Life interrupts the plan.

What matters is that you know how to get back on the apparatus, reset your grip, and keep going without losing form.

This final section focuses on exactly that.

Staying disciplined.

Staying protected.

Staying honest.

And winning over time.

# Chapter 25: Advisors, Scams, and Winning Over Time

Every gymnast remembers the first time a routine started to fall apart.

A small balance check turns into a wobble. The wobble turns into hesitation. The hesitation turns into a missed connection. Suddenly you are improvising instead of executing. From the outside it looks like nerves. From the inside, it feels like trying to save something that is already slipping.

That is what happens when athletes try to manage complex financial decisions alone for too long.

There is a point in every gymnastics career when self-coaching stops being enough. You still own the routine. You still do the work. But you need eyes on the outside. Someone who sees angles you cannot. Someone who helps you correct before mistakes turn into deductions.

Money works the same way.

Long-term success is not about doing everything yourself. It is about knowing when guidance protects you and when bad advice puts you at risk.

## *When to Seek Professional Help*

Gymnasts do not bring in specialists because they are failing. They bring them in because the routine is getting harder.

Financial help makes sense when:

- Your income increases or becomes more complex
- You have multiple accounts, investments, or benefits
- You are unsure how decisions interact with taxes, risk, or long-term goals
- You feel anxious, stuck, or reactive instead of confident
- You are making decisions that affect other people

In gymnastics terms, this is when difficulty increases.

Higher difficulty routines demand more precision. You do not guess on connections. You drill them. You spot them. You clean them up before competition.

Financial professionals are not there to take over your routine. They are there to help you execute it cleanly.

Waiting too long often costs more than getting help early.

## *Types of Financial Advisors*

Not all coaches coach the same events. Not all financial advisors do the same work.

Understanding the difference matters.

Some advisors focus only on investments.

Some focus on insurance.

Some focus on planning, coordination, and long-term strategy.

Key distinctions include:

- **Commission-based advisors** who are paid when products are sold
- **Fee-based or fee-only advisors** who are paid for advice and planning
- **Fiduciaries** who are legally required to act in your best interest

In gymnastics terms, this is knowing who is spotting you and why.

A spotter who gets paid only if you attempt harder skills may not prioritize safety. A coach who is paid to help you stick landings thinks differently.

The most important questions are not:

- "How confident do they sound?"
- "How impressive is their pitch?"

The important questions are:

- How are they paid?
- Who do they work for?
- Do they explain clearly?
- Do they slow you down when needed?
- Do they respect your goals, not just their strategy?

Good advisors educate. Bad ones impress.

## *Recognizing Scams and Bad Advice*

Gymnasts are taught early to recognize unsafe situations.

Bad mats.

Rushed warmups.

Pressure to throw skills you are not ready for.

Financial scams work the same way.

They rely on:

- Urgency
- Exclusivity
- Fear of missing out
- Flattery
- Complexity used to confuse, not clarify

Common red flags include:

- Guaranteed returns
- "Everyone is doing this"
- Pressure to act immediately

- Lack of transparency
- Discouraging second opinions

In gymnastics terms, this is being told to throw a skill without a proper warmup because "you've got it" or "trust me."

Real professionals welcome questions. Scams avoid them.

If something cannot be explained clearly, it is usually not safe.

## *Ten Common Financial Mistakes Athletes Make*

1. **Waiting too long to get organized**
2. Hoping things will sort themselves out rarely works.
3. **Chasing returns instead of building systems**
4. Difficulty without form leads to falls.
5. **Listening to the loudest voice in the room**
6. Confidence is not competence.
7. **Skipping protection to feel aggressive**
8. Ignoring safety increases injury risk.
9. **Confusing income with wealth**
10. High scores do not matter if you fall at the end.
11. **Overcomplicating early**
12. Basics before bonus points.
13. **Ignoring taxes and long-term impact**
14. Deductions show up later.
15. **Avoiding uncomfortable reviews**
16. Film study matters.
17. **Letting ego drive decisions**
18. Flash over form costs consistency.
19. **Assuming success will always continue**
20. Careers change. Bodies change. Markets change.

None of these mistakes happen because athletes are lazy. They happen because athletes are confident, competitive, and used to figuring things out under pressure.

Money punishes improvisation.

## *Ten Rules for Long-Term Success*

1. **Protect your base before adding difficulty**
2. Stability comes first.
3. **Build systems you can repeat under stress**
4. Consistency beats intensity.
5. **Ask for help earlier than you think you need it**
6. Prevention beats repair.
7. **Demand clarity, not hype**
8. If it sounds impressive but feels confusing, slow down.
9. **Understand how people are compensated**
10. Follow incentives.
11. **Review regularly, not reactively**
12. Scheduled check-ins prevent panic.
13. **Keep protection in place even when things feel good**
14. That is when risk increases.
15. **Separate confidence from capacity**
16. Feeling ready does not mean being ready.
17. **Make decisions that still work if things change**
18. Flexibility equals longevity.
19. **Think in seasons, not single meets**
20. Long careers are built one clean routine at a time.

## *Coach's Perspective*

A coach would not sugarcoat this.

Protect yourself.

Do not rush difficulty.

Ask for eyes when routines get harder.

Do not let ego override safety.

Finish strong.

You do not win by doing everything alone.

You win by staying upright when pressure hits.

## *Game Situations and Decision Points*

You are offered a financial opportunity that sounds exclusive.

Do you ask questions or rush to avoid missing out?

You feel overwhelmed managing everything yourself.

Do you seek guidance or keep guessing?

You hear conflicting advice from friends and social media.

Do you verify or react?

These moments decide outcomes.

## *Common Athlete Mistakes and Financial Parallels*

Athletes trust confidence over preparation.

Financially, that leads to bad advice.

Athletes push difficulty before form is ready.

Financially, that leads to losses.

Athletes avoid asking for help.

Financially, that leads to preventable mistakes.

## *Winning Over Time*

Long-term success is not about perfect routines.

It is about staying on the apparatus year after year.

It is about protecting what you build, correcting when needed, and refusing to let short-term pressure ruin long-term progress.

Gymnastics taught you how to train for this.

Money just asks you to apply it.

## *Athlete Takeaways*

- Get a spotter when difficulty increases
- Clear explanations beat impressive promises
- Protect your base before chasing upside
- Review regularly, not only after mistakes
- Long careers are built on clean execution, not hero saves

# Chapter 26: Losing the Schedule and Rebuilding Structure

Every gymnast remembers the day the schedule disappeared.

For years, your life was mapped out almost to the minute. Practice times. Warm-ups. Conditioning. Travel. Recovery. School blocks built around training. Someone else decided when you showed up, when you worked, and when you rested. You did not have to negotiate with yourself. The structure existed, and you lived inside it.

Then one day, it was gone.

No practice schedule on the wall.

No coach setting training times.

No competition calendar forcing preparation.

At first, the freedom feels good. You can sleep in. You can choose your day. You can finally relax.

Then things quietly start to slip.

Money behaves the same way.

When structure disappears, discipline becomes optional. Optional discipline rarely survives long-term.

## *Why Life Gets Harder When No One Is Setting Your Calendar*

Structure does more than organize time. It removes decision fatigue.

As a gymnast, you did not wake up each day asking:

- "Should I train today?"
- "How hard should I push?"
- "When should I stretch?"

Those decisions were already made. Your job was execution.

When the schedule disappears, everything requires a choice. When to wake up. When to work. When to save. When to spend. When to plan. When to review.

Most people underestimate how exhausting that is.

In gymnastics terms, this is being asked to design your own training plan, judge your own routines, and decide when competition is close enough to matter. Without structure, even disciplined athletes start drifting.

Money feels harder not because you are worse at it, but because no one is setting the cadence anymore.

### *From Mandatory Workouts to Optional Discipline*

Mandatory workouts create consistency even on bad days.

Optional workouts rely on motivation.

Motivation is unreliable.

Financial habits work the same way. When saving, budgeting, and reviewing are optional, they slowly disappear. Not all at once. Quietly.

You miss one review.

Then another.

Then a month goes by.

Nothing explodes immediately, so it feels fine. But underneath, habits are weakening.

In gymnastics, this is skipping basics because you feel advanced. The routine may hold for a while. Then execution suffers when pressure returns.

Discipline without structure becomes fragile.

## *How Lack of Structure Quietly Breaks Financial Habits*

Most financial problems do not come from one bad decision. They come from erosion.

No set time to check accounts.

No regular saving cadence.

No review of goals.

No awareness of spending patterns.

Without structure, money becomes reactive. Bills get paid late. Savings happen only when there is extra. Decisions are made emotionally instead of intentionally.

In gymnastics terms, this is losing your rhythm. The skills are still there, but the routine feels rushed, disconnected, and sloppy.

You are not failing. You are just unstructured.

## *The Illusion of "I'll Get to It Later"*

Athletes are especially vulnerable to this trap.

You are used to pushing through. You believe you can always clean things up later. You trust your ability to recover.

But money punishes delay.

Missed savings reps do not come back.

Unreviewed habits compound quietly.

Bad structure shows up years later, not immediately.

In gymnastics, you cannot cram flexibility the week before a meet. Financial habits work the same way.

Later is expensive.

## *Replacing Practice Schedules With Personal Systems*

When formal training ends, successful gymnasts replace it with personal systems.

You decide:

- When you train
- How you condition
- How you recover
- How you maintain fundamentals

Money requires the same shift.

You must replace external structure with internal systems.

This does not mean complicated spreadsheets or perfect tracking. It means predictable routines.

Examples include:

- A set day each week to review accounts
- Automatic savings scheduled like practice
- Monthly check-ins with yourself or a professional
- Annual goal-setting tied to real timelines

In gymnastics terms, this is self-coached training. The routine may be simpler, but consistency matters more than difficulty.

Systems beat motivation every time.

## *Why Simple Systems Work Best*

Athletes often overcomplicate this phase.

They build elaborate plans they cannot sustain. When life gets busy, the system collapses.

Coaches never design routines athletes cannot repeat under pressure. Your financial systems should follow the same rule.

Simple systems:

- Run automatically
- Require minimal decision-making
- Still work on bad days

Complex systems fail when stress shows up.

Clean execution matters more than impressive design.

## *Time Blocking and Financial Rhythm*

Gymnastics teaches rhythm.

You know when to accelerate. When to pause. When to reset. Money needs rhythm too.

Without designated time for money, it gets pushed to the background. When money finally demands attention, it shows up as stress.

Blocking time for financial basics creates calm:

- A weekly review creates awareness
- A monthly reset maintains alignment
- An annual review sets direction

In gymnastics terms, this is choreographing your routine so nothing feels rushed.

## *Structure Is Freedom, Not Restriction*

Many athletes resist structure because it feels like losing freedom.

In reality, structure creates freedom.

When basics are handled automatically:

- You worry less
- You react less
- You make better decisions

That is why structured training produces confident athletes. The same applies to money.

Structure removes noise.

## *Coach's Perspective*

A coach would be blunt.

Nobody is coming to save you.

Optional discipline is not discipline.

If it matters, schedule it.

Reps do not happen by accident.

Build systems or accept drift.

This is not about perfection. It is about showing up consistently.

## *Game Situations and Decision Points*

You no longer have a set routine for money.

Do you build one or hope motivation shows up?

You feel behind financially.

Do you add structure or avoid the numbers?

You have freedom but feel scattered.

Do you design systems or keep reacting?

The answer is always structure.

## *Common Athlete Mistakes and Financial Parallels*

Athletes rely on motivation.

Financially, that leads to inconsistency.

Athletes skip basics once competition ends.

Financially, that leads to erosion.

Athletes assume discipline will appear later.

Financially, that leads to regret.

### *Winning the Long Game*

The best gymnasts learn this lesson early.

Structure does not limit creativity. It supports it.

When your foundation is solid, you can take risks intentionally. When your systems are in place, freedom becomes real.

Money is no different.

You are not losing discipline. You are losing structure.

Rebuild it on purpose.

### *Athlete Takeaways*

- When the schedule disappears, systems must replace it
- Optional discipline fades fast without structure
- Simple systems beat complicated plans
- Schedule money like you scheduled practice
- Long-term success comes from consistent routines, not bursts of effort

# Chapter 27: From Teammates to Coworkers

Every gymnast remembers the feeling of being part of a team, even in an individual sport.

You trained side by side. You warmed up together. You shared chalk, nerves, and inside jokes. Even when routines were judged individually, the environment was collective. Coaches knew your strengths and weaknesses. Teammates understood the grind. Expectations were mostly clear, even when pressure was high.

Then the uniform comes off.

Suddenly, you are in a workplace where none of that context exists. No one knows how hard you trained. No one cares how many hours you spent perfecting basics. The discipline that once earned respect is invisible unless you translate it into a new environment.

This transition is one of the most overlooked challenges former athletes face, and it has a direct impact on income growth, career stability, and long-term financial success.

## *Why the Workplace Feels Foreign After Sports*

Sports environments are structured, direct, and performance-based.

Workplaces are not.

In gymnastics, expectations were clear:

- Show up on time
- Train hard
- Execute the routine
- Accept feedback
- Improve

In many workplaces, expectations are implied instead of stated. Success is measured indirectly. Feedback is inconsistent. Performance reviews happen infrequently and are often vague.

That gap creates confusion, especially for athletes who thrived in environments with clarity and accountability.

You are not worse at working. You are adjusting to a completely different system.

### *Authority Without Coaches*

In sports, authority is obvious.

The coach sets the tone. The rules are enforced. Feedback is immediate. If something goes wrong, you know exactly who to listen to and what needs to change.

In the workplace, authority is layered.

You may have:

- A manager
- A team lead
- An HR department
- Unwritten power structures

Not all authority figures coach. Some manage. Some avoid conflict. Some communicate indirectly.

For former gymnasts, this feels disorienting. You are used to being corrected loudly and clearly. Silence can feel like approval when it is actually indifference.

Financially, this matters because unclear authority leads to missed opportunities. Raises, promotions, and role clarity often require asking questions and advocating for yourself. Waiting to be coached can stall income growth.

### *Feedback Without Film*

Gymnastics teaches you to live on film.

Every routine is reviewed. Every mistake is visible. Progress is measurable. Feedback is specific. You know what stuck and what did not.

Most workplaces do not operate this way.

Feedback may be:

- Delayed
- General
- Softened
- Avoided

You may not know how you are performing until a review months later. You may be told you are "doing fine" without direction. That lack of clarity creates anxiety for athletes who are wired to adjust quickly.

Without feedback, athletes may:

- Overwork unnecessarily
- Second-guess decisions
- Assume poor performance
- Or disengage completely

From a money perspective, this uncertainty affects confidence. Confidence affects negotiation, career moves, and long-term earning potential.

## *Politics, Ambiguity, and Unclear Expectations*

Gymnastics is brutally honest.

You either stay on the apparatus or you do not. Scores are visible. Results are public.

Workplaces are political by nature.

Decisions are influenced by relationships, perception, timing, and internal dynamics that have nothing to do with raw performance. This is not good or bad. It is reality.

Former athletes often struggle here because politics feel unfair. You are used to merit-based systems. You assume effort and results speak for themselves.

In many workplaces, they do not.

Understanding workplace dynamics is not selling out. It is learning the new game.

Ignoring this reality can:

- Limit advancement
- Create frustration
- Stall compensation growth
- Increase job instability

Athletes who refuse to adapt often feel stuck despite working hard.

## *Losing the Built-In Team Identity*

Gymnastics provided identity.

You knew who you were. A gymnast. A teammate. A competitor. That identity gave structure and belonging.

Workplaces rarely replace that automatically.

Coworkers may be friendly, but they are not teammates in the same way. Everyone has different incentives, goals, and pressures. Loyalty is conditional. Turnover is normal.

This can feel isolating, especially for athletes used to tight-knit environments.

Isolation often leads to poor financial decisions:

- Staying in bad jobs too long
- Avoiding negotiation
- Accepting underpayment
- Chasing validation through spending

Money mistakes often show up during identity transitions, not because of ignorance, but because of emotional stress.

## *Translating Athletic Skills Into Workplace Value*

The mistake many athletes make is assuming employers automatically understand their background.

They do not.

Discipline, resilience, and work ethic only matter if they are translated into results the organization values.

That requires learning a new language:

- Outcomes instead of effort
- Communication instead of assumption
- Visibility instead of silent grind

This translation directly affects income growth. Promotions and raises are not awarded for potential. They are awarded for perceived impact.

Gymnastics taught you how to master fundamentals. The workplace requires you to apply those fundamentals differently.

## *How This Impacts Income Growth*

Income growth is rarely linear.

Athletes often expect:

- Work hard
- Improve
- Get rewarded

In reality, income growth often requires:

- Strategic job moves
- Clear communication of value
- Negotiation
- Understanding timing

Without understanding workplace dynamics, athletes may under-earn for years.

This is not a motivation issue. It is a systems issue.

Once you understand the new environment, your discipline becomes an advantage again.

## *Career Stability and Financial Stress*

Unclear expectations create stress. Stress leads to reactive decisions.

Athletes under workplace stress may:

- Avoid long-term planning
- Delay saving and investing
- Take on unnecessary debt
- Chase income without stability

Career instability and financial instability reinforce each other.

Learning how to navigate the workplace is not just about job satisfaction. It is about protecting your financial foundation.

### *Coach's Perspective*

A coach would reframe the situation.

Different arena. Same fundamentals.

Learn the rules before judging the game.

Ask questions instead of guessing.

Effort matters, but awareness matters more.

If you want minutes, understand the system.

You are not starting over. You are adapting.

### *Game Situations and Decision Points*

You are unsure how you are performing.

Do you ask for feedback or assume?

You feel underpaid.

Do you prepare to negotiate or wait to be noticed?

You dislike workplace politics.

Do you disengage or learn to navigate them?

These decisions shape both career and financial outcomes.

### *Common Athlete Mistakes and Financial Parallels*

Athletes expect coaching without asking.

Financially, that leads to stalled income.

Athletes avoid uncomfortable conversations.

Financially, that leads to under-earning.

Athletes confuse effort with visibility.

Financially, that leads to missed opportunities.

## *Winning the Long Game*

The best former gymnasts learn to rebuild teams differently.

They find mentors.

They build professional networks.

They create structure where none exists.

They stop waiting for coaches and start managing their own development.

That shift unlocks both career stability and financial confidence.

## *Athlete Takeaways*

- The workplace is a different system, not a worse one
- Authority and feedback are indirect and must be sought
- Politics exist whether you like them or not
- Income growth requires communication and strategy
- Adaptation turns discipline back into an advantage

# Chapter 28: When No One Is Watching Anymore

Every gymnast knows this moment.

The meet is over. The judges' tables are being cleared. Teammates are changing out of their leotards. The lights dim. The adrenaline fades. What remains is silence.

No scores.

No crowd.

No coach clapping or correcting.

No one watching.

For years, your discipline lived inside visibility. Training schedules. Practice times. Lineups. Meets. Consequences were immediate. Accountability was built into the system.

Then one day, that system disappears.

And that is where many former athletes struggle, not because they lost discipline, but because the environment that enforced it is gone.

Money mistakes often begin right here.

## *The Discipline Gap After Accountability Disappears*

Gymnastics does not allow casual effort.

If you skip basics, it shows.

If you rush progressions, it shows.

If you lack consistency, it shows.

Accountability is constant. Even when no one says anything, the apparatus does.

Adult life is different.

You can:

- Skip saving for months
- Ignore credit card balances
- Avoid checking accounts
- Delay investing
- Overspend quietly

And nothing happens right away.

No whistle.

No deduction.

No one pulls you aside.

That delay creates a discipline gap.

Without immediate feedback, habits slowly loosen. What felt temporary becomes permanent. What felt harmless compounds.

This is not a character flaw. It is a system change.

### *Why Former Athletes Self-Sabotage Without Pressure*

Athletes are trained to perform under pressure.

Deadlines.

Competition.

Evaluation.

Remove pressure, and motivation often fades. Not because you became lazy, but because your brain was conditioned to respond to stakes.

Money rarely creates visible stakes early.

You can overspend today and feel fine.

You can avoid saving this year and feel fine.

You can ignore planning in your 20s and feel fine.

Until you do not.

Former athletes often self-sabotage financially by:

- Waiting for urgency instead of building habits
- Confusing freedom with lack of structure
- Assuming discipline will magically transfer

Discipline does not disappear. It needs a new container.

## *Comfort vs Growth Decisions*

Gymnastics constantly forces growth decisions.
Do you:

- Stay with a skill that feels safe?
- Or push difficulty knowing you might fall?

Those decisions are guided by coaches, progressions, and long-term planning.
In adult life, no one guides those choices.
Comfort becomes tempting.
Comfort looks like:

- Spending instead of saving
- Convenience instead of intention
- Familiar jobs instead of growth opportunities
- Avoiding uncomfortable financial conversations

Growth requires friction.
Saving feels restrictive.
Investing feels uncertain.
Budgeting feels boring.
Learning taxes feels intimidating.
Without external pressure, comfort wins by default.

And comfort is expensive.

## *Translating "Grind Culture" Into Adult Life*

Athletes know how to grind.

Early mornings.

Late nights.

Reps when tired.

Pain tolerance.

But grind culture alone does not build wealth.

Grinding without direction becomes burnout.

Effort without structure becomes wasted motion.

In gymnastics, effort is guided.

Reps have purpose.

Progressions matter.

In adult life, grind must evolve into systems.

Financial grind without systems looks like:

- Working harder but not getting ahead
- Earning more but saving the same
- Hustling without building stability

The discipline that once built routines must now build habits.

## *Why Money Mistakes Show Up Years Later*

Gymnastics is unforgiving.

Mistakes show immediately.

Money is patient.

You can make small financial mistakes for years before consequences appear:

- Not investing early

- Carrying balances
- Ignoring insurance
- Skipping retirement contributions

The damage is delayed, not denied.

That delay is dangerous for athletes used to instant feedback.

By the time consequences appear, the gap feels overwhelming. That is why many people panic in their 30s and 40s and assume they failed.

They did not fail.

They drifted.

## *The Illusion of "I'll Fix It Later"*

Later feels infinite when you are young.

Athletes often believe:

- Income will always increase
- Motivation will return
- Time will be available
- Problems will be easier to fix

Gymnastics teaches the opposite.

You know that missed basics compound.

You know that flexibility lost is harder to regain.

You know that waiting costs more than effort.

Money works the same way.

Later is more expensive.

## *Building Internal Accountability*

When no one is watching, you must become the system.

That means:

- Scheduled money check-ins
- Automatic savings
- Clear rules for spending
- Written goals
- External accountability partners

You do not wait to feel motivated.

You build structure that works even when motivation disappears.

That is what elite athletes already know how to do.

They just need to apply it differently.

## *Financial Systems Replace External Pressure*

In gymnastics:

- The schedule created discipline
- The coach enforced it
- The meet tested it

In adult life:

- Systems create discipline
- Automation enforces it
- Time tests it

Budgets.

Automatic transfers.

Investment plans.

Regular reviews.

These are not restrictions.

They are replacement structures.

## *Coach's Perspective*

A coach would not sugarcoat this.

Nobody is coming to save you.

Comfort is the enemy.

If no one is watching, that's when it matters most.

Champions are built when nobody's watching.

Do not cheat the work.

Discipline without supervision is the real test.

## *Game Situations and Decision Points*

No one checks your spending.

Do you check it anyway?

You feel tired of being disciplined.

Do you ease off or simplify the system?

You are doing "fine."

Do you build habits or wait for urgency?

These are quiet moments.

They shape outcomes.

## *Common Athlete Mistakes and Financial Parallels*

Athletes rely on pressure to perform.

Financially, that leads to drifting.

Athletes equate grind with progress.

Financially, that leads to burnout without growth.

Athletes delay uncomfortable basics.

Financially, that leads to long-term regret.

## *Winning the Long Game*

The most successful former athletes learn this truth:

Discipline is not about intensity.

It is about consistency when no one is watching.

They stop relying on adrenaline.

They stop waiting for deadlines.

They stop assuming effort alone is enough.

They build systems.

They protect habits.

They trust boring consistency.

That is how they win long after the last routine.

## *Athlete Takeaways*

- Discipline must move from external to internal
- Comfort quietly costs more than effort
- Grind without systems leads to burnout
- Small money mistakes compound silently
- Build structure that works when no one is watching

# Chapter 29: Redefining Winning After the Uniform Comes Off

Every athlete remembers what winning used to mean.

A higher score.

A podium finish.

A scholarship.

A starting spot.

A championship banner.

Winning was visible. Measurable. Public. You knew exactly where you stood because the scoreboard told you. Coaches reinforced it. Teammates lived it with you. Your identity was tied to performance, and performance had clear metrics.

Then the uniform comes off.

And the scoreboard disappears.

What replaces it is not clarity. It is noise.

## *Why Chasing Status Replaces Chasing Performance*

When the structure of sport ends, many former athletes still want to win. That instinct never goes away. The problem is not ambition. The problem is misdirection.

Without a clear scoreboard, winning quietly morphs into status chasing.

Status is visible.

Performance is not.

Status looks like:

- Job titles
- Income numbers
- Houses
- Cars
- Vacations
- Lifestyle upgrades
- Social media highlights

Performance looks like:

- Stability
- Optionality
- Peace of mind
- Health
- Relationships
- Purpose
- Control over time

In gymnastics, you never confused flash for execution. A skill only counted if it was landed cleanly. In adult life, many athletes forget that rule.

They start chasing what looks impressive instead of what actually works.

## *Income vs Fulfillment*

Income is easy to measure.

Fulfillment is not.

That makes income tempting as a replacement scoreboard.

More income feels like winning.

Less income feels like losing.

But income alone is a weak metric.

You can earn a lot and:

- Feel trapped
- Hate your schedule
- Live paycheck to paycheck
- Carry constant stress
- Sacrifice health and relationships

In gymnastics terms, this is chasing difficulty without control. The score might look high for a moment, but the routine does not hold.

Fulfillment is harder to quantify, but it is more durable.

It shows up as:

- Work you do not dread
- Financial margin
- Time flexibility
- Alignment between values and decisions
- Confidence about the future

True winning balances income and fulfillment, not one at the expense of the other.

## *Titles, Houses, Cars, and Comparison Traps*

Comparison never left sports. It just changed uniforms.

Instead of comparing scores, you compare:

- Promotions
- Salaries
- Job titles
- Homes
- Vehicles
- Lifestyles

These comparisons are constant and subtle.

The danger is not noticing success around you.

The danger is letting it redefine your definition of winning.

Many former athletes buy things not because they need them, but because they feel behind. That feeling often has nothing to do with reality and everything to do with comparison.

In gymnastics, you did not change routines mid-meet because another gymnast hit a skill. You trusted your training.

Money deserves the same discipline.

## *The Hidden Cost of Status Chasing*

Status is expensive.

It creates:

- Lifestyle inflation
- Unnecessary debt
- Pressure to maintain appearances
- Decisions made for optics, not outcomes

Status also moves the goalposts.

There is always someone ahead.

Always someone earning more.

Always someone posting better highlights.

That chase never ends.

Performance-based winning does end.

It stabilizes.

It compounds.

## *What "Success" Actually Looks Like in Your 30s and 40s*

Success evolves.

In your teens and twenties, success often means proving yourself.

In your thirties and forties, success often means protecting yourself.

That shift is uncomfortable for athletes who were trained to push, not preserve.

Real success later looks like:

- The ability to say no
- Financial margin for mistakes
- A career that does not consume your identity
- Time for family, health, and purpose
- Less anxiety about money, not more

In gymnastics terms, this is longevity. Clean execution. Staying healthy enough to keep competing.

You stop chasing perfect scores.

You focus on sticking the landing.

## *Why Athletes Feel "Lost" After Early Success*

Many athletes experience success early in life.

Recognition.

Praise.

Structure.

Validation.

Then adulthood feels flat.

Workplaces do not celebrate effort.

Progress is slower.

Feedback is vague.

Rewards are delayed.

That creates confusion.

Athletes often assume they failed because life feels harder.

They did not fail.

The metrics changed.

Winning is no longer external.

It is internal.

## *Building a New Scoreboard*

You need a new way to measure success.

Not one borrowed from social media.

Not one borrowed from coworkers.

Not one borrowed from your past self.

A personal scoreboard might include:

- Net worth growth over time
- Savings rate
- Debt reduction
- Time flexibility
- Career satisfaction
- Health consistency
- Relationships maintained
- Stress levels

These metrics are quieter.

They are also more honest.

In gymnastics, you learned to judge your own execution before the judges posted scores. That internal standard is exactly what adult life requires.

## *Redefining Competition*

Competition does not disappear after sports.

It turns inward.

The healthiest competitors stop trying to beat others and start trying to outperform their past selves.

Financial competition becomes:

- Better habits this year than last
- More margin than before
- Fewer reactive decisions

- Greater alignment with values

That is a game you can actually win.

### *Letting Go of Who You Used to Be*

This is the hardest part.

Athletes often cling to past versions of themselves:

- The starter
- The champion
- The standout

That identity served you then.

It may limit you now.

Redefining winning requires releasing outdated scoreboards.

You are not losing.

You are evolving.

### *Coach's Perspective*

A coach would say it directly.

Stop comparing.

Play your game.

Know what winning looks like for you.

Do not chase noise.

Finish strong.

No one cares about the flash if the routine falls apart at the end.

### *Game Situations and Decision Points*

You are offered more money but less flexibility.

Do you evaluate fulfillment or just income?

You feel behind because someone else upgraded their lifestyle.

Do you respond emotionally or check your own scoreboard?

You hit a milestone you thought would feel better.

Do you reflect or chase the next thing immediately?

These decisions define adulthood the same way routines defined competition.

### *Common Athlete Mistakes and Financial Parallels*

Athletes chase recognition.

Financially, that becomes status spending.

Athletes confuse difficulty with quality.

Financially, that becomes complexity without purpose.

Athletes fear slowing down.

Financially, that leads to burnout and regret.

### *Winning the Long Game*

Winning after sports is not louder.

It is quieter.

It feels like control.

It feels like confidence.

It feels like choice.

The athletes who succeed long-term are not the ones who replaced medals with money. They are the ones who replaced scoreboards with values.

They stop asking, "How do I look?"

They start asking, "How does this hold up over time?"

That is real winning.

## *Athlete Takeaways*

- Status is not performance
- Income without fulfillment is a weak scoreboard
- Comparison distorts decision-making
- Success evolves with age and priorities
- Build a personal scoreboard and stick the landing

# Chapter 30: Staying Connected Without Living in the Past

Every gymnast remembers the feeling of being part of something bigger.

The team warm-up.

The shared nerves before competition.

The quiet focus in the gym.

The unspoken understanding that everyone around you was chasing the same standard.

That environment was not just about performance. It was about belonging.

When gymnastics ends, that belonging often disappears overnight.

No more shared schedules.

No more teammates who understand your sacrifices.

No more coaches setting expectations.

No more locker room, gym floor, or place where you automatically fit.

That loss is subtle, but it is powerful.

## *The Role of Community, Mentorship, and New Locker Rooms*

Gymnastics did not just train your body. It trained your identity.

You knew where to go.

You knew who you were accountable to.

You knew what mattered that day.

After sports, many athletes assume they need to become independent and move on alone. That belief creates isolation.

The truth is simpler.

You never succeeded alone in gymnastics.

You will not thrive alone after it.

Community does not disappear. It changes form.

New locker rooms exist in:

- Careers
- Professional networks
- Friend groups
- Mentorship relationships
- Service, coaching, or leadership roles

The mistake is waiting for them to appear automatically.

You have to seek them out.

## *Why Isolation Hits Former Athletes Hard*

Former athletes are especially vulnerable to isolation for one reason.

You were surrounded by people every day for years.

Then suddenly, you are not.

Work environments are transactional.

Friendships require effort.

Schedules are unstructured.

No one checks if you showed up.

That shift feels like failure when it is actually transition.

Isolation often shows up as:

- Loss of motivation
- Disconnection from purpose
- Overworking or underworking
- Emotional numbness

- Using money, work, or status to fill the gap

This is not weakness.

It is the absence of structure and shared mission.

Gymnastics gave you both.

Life does not hand them out automatically.

### *Finding Purpose Without the Team*

Purpose used to be obvious.

Train.

Compete.

Improve.

Support the team.

After sports, purpose feels abstract.

Many former athletes chase purpose through achievement.

Others chase it through distraction.

Neither works long-term.

Purpose after sports comes from contribution.

Contribution looks like:

- Helping others
- Teaching what you know
- Building something meaningful
- Leading, mentoring, or supporting

In gymnastics terms, this is becoming the upperclassman who sets the tone instead of chasing scores.

Purpose is not found.

It is built.

## *Healthy Nostalgia vs Being Stuck*

Nostalgia is natural.

You should remember the good moments.

You should be proud of what you did.

You should honor the part of your life that shaped you.

The danger is confusing nostalgia with identity.

Healthy nostalgia:

- Appreciates the past
- Learns from it
- Integrates it into who you are now

Being stuck:

- Replays the past
- Compares the present to it
- Uses it to avoid moving forward

If every good memory makes today feel smaller, nostalgia has crossed into stagnation.

Gymnastics was a chapter.

Not the whole book.

## *Creating a Forward-Looking Identity*

The hardest shift for former athletes is answering one question.

Who am I now?

That question feels threatening because gymnastics gave you clarity.

Taking it away feels like losing yourself.

You did not lose yourself.

You expanded.

Your discipline still matters.

Your work ethic still matters.

Your standards still matter.

They just apply to new arenas.

A forward-looking identity:

- Uses athletic traits in new ways
- Builds new goals instead of reliving old ones
- Values growth over recognition
- Allows multiple roles instead of one label

You are not "former."

You are evolving.

## *Replacing the Team Environment Intentionally*

You cannot replace gymnastics.

You can replace the environment that supported you.

That means:

- Seeking mentors instead of waiting for coaches
- Building routines instead of relying on schedules
- Creating accountability instead of expecting it
- Finding communities that challenge and support you

This takes effort.

It is worth it.

The athletes who struggle the most are not the ones who miss gymnastics.

They are the ones who never replace the environment it gave them.

## *Why Money Gets Tied to Identity*

Many former athletes use money to fill connection gaps.
Spending creates temporary excitement.
Status creates temporary validation.
Work creates temporary structure.
None of these replace belonging.
When community is missing, money decisions become emotional.
When connection is strong, money becomes a tool again.
Your financial health is closely tied to your social health.

## *Coach's Perspective*

A coach would say this clearly.
Do not isolate.
Find your people.
Stay connected.
Move forward.
Do not live in yesterday.
Championship teams evolve.
So do athletes.

## *Game Situations and Decision Points*

You feel disconnected from your past teammates.
Do you isolate or seek new community?
You miss the structure of the gym.
Do you drift or build routines?
You find yourself reliving old moments.
Do you honor them or hide in them?
These decisions shape life after sports.

## *Common Athlete Mistakes and Financial Parallels*

Athletes isolate when structure disappears.
Financially, that leads to emotional decisions.
Athletes cling to old identities.
Financially, that leads to chasing status.
Athletes avoid building new communities.
Financially, that leads to using money for validation.

## *Winning the Long Game*

Life after gymnastics is not about replacing the past.
It is about building the next phase with intention.
You do not need the same team.
You need connection.
You do not need the same scoreboard.
You need purpose.
The athletes who thrive long-term stay connected without staying stuck.
They honor where they came from.
They invest in where they are going.
That is how you finish strong.

## *Athlete Takeaways*

- Community matters long after competition ends
- Isolation quietly erodes motivation and discipline
- Nostalgia is healthy only if it does not trap you
- Purpose comes from contribution, not comparison
- Build new locker rooms and move forward with intention

# Glossary of Gymnastics and Financial Terms

This glossary connects key financial concepts to familiar ideas from **gymnastics**, making money easier to understand through the language, structure, and discipline gymnasts already know.

## *Asset Allocation*

**Financial Definition:**

How money is divided among different investment types such as stocks, bonds, and cash to balance risk and return.

**Gymnastics Comparison:**

How difficulty, balance, and timing are distributed across events and skills. Too much focus on difficulty without control increases the chance of a fall.

## *Assets*

**Financial Definition:**

Things you own that have value, such as cash, investments, real estate, or retirement accounts.

**Gymnastics Comparison:**

Your strengths as a gymnast: skills, conditioning, flexibility, experience, and preparation that contribute to overall performance.

### *Bonds*

**Financial Definition:**

Loans made to governments or companies that pay interest and return principal over time.

**Gymnastics Comparison:**

The base and form of a routine. Not flashy, but essential for stability and control when pressure increases.

### *Budget*

**Financial Definition:**

A plan for how income is allocated toward expenses, savings, and goals.

**Gymnastics Comparison:**

Routine choreography and counts. Without knowing the sequence and timing, execution breaks down.

### *Cash Flow*

**Financial Definition:**

Money coming in versus money going out.

**Gymnastics Comparison:**

Energy management across a routine. Burn too much early and you struggle to finish strong.

### *Compounding*

**Financial Definition:**

Earnings that generate additional earnings over time.

**Gymnastics Comparison:**

Daily reps and muscle memory. Each repetition builds on the last and makes progress feel easier over time.

*Credit*

**Financial Definition:**

The ability to borrow money with the promise of repayment.

**Gymnastics Comparison:**

Trust from coaches and judges. When earned and managed well, it allows advancement. When abused, it creates risk.

*Debt*

**Financial Definition:**

Money borrowed that must be repaid, often with interest.

**Gymnastics Comparison:**

Added weight or difficulty. Manageable in small amounts, dangerous when excessive.

*Diversification*

**Financial Definition:**

Spreading investments across different assets to reduce risk.

**Gymnastics Comparison:**

Not relying on one skill or one event to carry your entire score. Balance across events protects the total outcome.

*Emergency Fund*

**Financial Definition:**

Savings set aside for unexpected expenses.

**Gymnastics Comparison:**

Spotters and safety mats. You hope you never need them, but they prevent major setbacks when something goes wrong.

### *ETF (Exchange-Traded Fund)*

**Financial Definition:**

A fund that holds many investments and trades like a stock.

**Gymnastics Comparison:**

A team routine instead of a solo skill. Shared responsibility reduces risk.

### *Fees / Expense Ratios*

**Financial Definition:**

Costs associated with managing investments.

**Gymnastics Comparison:**

Execution deductions. Small penalties that quietly lower your final score over time.

### *Growth Investing*

**Financial Definition:**

Investing in companies expected to grow faster than average.

**Gymnastics Comparison:**

Higher difficulty skills. More upside, but only effective when fundamentals are solid.

### *Insurance*

**Financial Definition:**

Protection against financial loss from unexpected events.

**Gymnastics Comparison:**

Safety equipment and injury prevention. You do not perform without protection when risk increases.

*Liquidity*

**Financial Definition:**

How easily money can be accessed without penalty or delay.

**Gymnastics Comparison:**

Flexibility to adjust mid-routine when something feels off.

*Net Worth*

**Financial Definition:**

Assets minus liabilities.

**Gymnastics Comparison:**

Your overall meet score. Not one skill, but the complete performance.

*Rebalancing*

**Financial Definition:**

Adjusting investments back to their intended mix over time.

**Gymnastics Comparison:**

Mid-season corrections to restore balance, form, and consistency.

*Risk*

**Financial Definition:**

The chance that outcomes differ from expectations, including loss.

**Gymnastics Comparison:**

Difficulty selection. Higher reward comes with higher risk of deduction or fall.

## *Roth IRA*

**Financial Definition:**

A retirement account where money grows tax-free if rules are followed.

**Gymnastics Comparison:**

Front-loaded discipline so the landing is cleaner later in the routine.

## *Stocks*

**Financial Definition:**

Ownership shares in a company.

**Gymnastics Comparison:**

High-difficulty elements. They drive scoring potential but need strong support to succeed.

## *Tax-Advantaged Accounts*

**Financial Definition:**

Accounts that provide tax benefits, often with rules and restrictions.

**Gymnastics Comparison:**

Structured training plans. Rules exist to improve long-term results, not limit progress.

## *Volatility*

**Financial Definition:**

Short-term ups and downs in market value.

**Gymnastics Comparison:**

A wobble. Normal movement that only becomes a problem if you panic.

### *Permanent Loss*

**Financial Definition:**

Money that cannot recover due to poor decisions or panic.

**Gymnastics Comparison:**

A fall. Usually caused by abandoning fundamentals under pressure.

### *Total Return*

**Financial Definition:**

Investment return from both price growth and income.

**Gymnastics Comparison:**

The full routine score. Difficulty, execution, and landing all matter.

### *Value Investing*

**Financial Definition:**

Investing in assets believed to be undervalued.

**Gymnastics Comparison:**

Clean execution. Less flash, more control, consistent results.

### *Yield*

**Financial Definition:**

Income generated from an investment.

**Gymnastics Comparison:**

Consistent scoring. Not dramatic, but reliable and repeatable.

### *Final Note*

This glossary reinforces one core principle:

Financial success, like success in **gymnastics**, comes from balance, discipline, timing, and repetition.

That philosophy runs through **Gymnastics Money 101** and continues long after competition ends.

# Disclaimers

**Educational Purpose Only**

This book is for educational purposes only.

The information provided in **Gymnastics Money 101** is intended to help readers understand general financial concepts using gymnastics-based analogies. It is not individualized financial, investment, tax, legal, or insurance advice.

Every financial situation is different. Your goals, income, family circumstances, risk tolerance, and time horizon are unique. What works for one person may not be appropriate for another.

## Not Financial, Investment, or Legal Advice

Nothing in this book should be interpreted as a recommendation to buy, sell, or hold any specific investment, financial product, or strategy.

This book does not replace advice from qualified professionals such as:

- Financial advisors
- Accountants or tax professionals
- Attorneys
- Insurance professionals

Before making financial decisions, readers should consult professionals who can evaluate their individual situation.

## No Guarantees or Promises of Results

All investing involves risk, including the possible loss of principal.

Past performance does not guarantee future results. Markets fluctuate. Economic conditions change. Outcomes cannot be predicted or guaranteed.

The examples and scenarios in this book are illustrative only and may not reflect actual results or real-world outcomes.

## Tax and Legal Information

Any discussion of taxes, retirement accounts, estate planning, or legal structures is general in nature.

Tax laws and regulations change frequently and vary by jurisdiction. Legal requirements differ based on location and personal circumstances.

Readers should seek personalized tax or legal advice before acting on any information related to these topics.

## Athlete and Career Considerations

This book discusses financial topics as they relate to athletes and former athletes, including career transitions and income changes.

It does not provide career placement services, employment advice, or guarantees related to income, compensation, or career success.

## Use of Analogies

Gymnastics and sports analogies are used to make financial concepts easier to understand.

These analogies are educational tools only and should not be interpreted literally. Financial decisions require analysis beyond analogy.

## Personal Responsibility

By reading this book, you acknowledge that:

- You are responsible for your own financial decisions
- You understand that financial outcomes involve uncertainty
- You agree to seek appropriate professional guidance when needed

Education improves decision-making, but responsibility remains with the individual.

## Contact Information

If you would like to learn more about the concepts discussed in this book or explore additional educational resources, **Pat Brown** can be found through public platforms including LinkedIn, Twitter, and via Google search.

For questions specifically related to **Gymnastics Money 101**, you may contact Pat Brown at:

**info@gymnasticsmoney101.com**

## Final Reminder

Financial success is built over time through discipline, planning, and consistency.

This book provides a framework, not a guarantee.

Use it as a guide, not a substitute for professional advice.

*Pat Brown OLB, University of Kansas*

Made in the USA
Monee, IL
04 November 2026

67386755R00148